A WORLD
THAT'S
ALL OUR OWN.....

Published by Cynthia Morey

Publishing partner: Paragon Publishing, Rothersthorpe

First published 2006

© Cynthia Morey 2006

Cover photograph: from the Leamington & Warwick Operatic
Society production of *The Pirates of Penzance* 1949

ISBN 1-899820-28-0 Paperback

Book design, layout and production management by Into Print

www.intoprint.net

Printed and bound in UK and USA by Lightning Source

'A WORLD THAT'S ALL OUR OWN.....'

This story was written way back in 1984, when I was in 'Me and My Girl' at the Adelphi Theatre. It began life as a play. I had great fun writing it, and colleagues from the show came and recorded it amid much laughter and countless cups of coffee. I showed the manuscript to a literary agent who liked it very much, but it soon became clear that the play would require too large a cast to make it commercially viable. So it lay on a shelf, gathering dust while I turned to more important activities.

A few years ago, while engaging in some belated spring clean-ing, I came upon the manuscript, read it again, and decided it might convert into a novel. I set to work on the re-writing, but at this point more pressing things once again intervened, and back on the shelf it went. Earlier this year I discovered the manuscript once again and decided it was really time to do something about it or consign it to the recycling bin. So here it is.

There are no murders, no crime and no violence in my story; it's just a peep behind the scenes as an amateur operatic society puts on its annual production. Do I have first-hand knowledge of such things? You bet!

Before embarking on my professional career in the theatre I belonged to several amateur societies, and in later years I have directed a number of such performances- particularly Gilbert and Sullivan productions. And I don't mind telling you that what goes on behind the scenes is sometimes more dramatic than the action on stage!

I am glad that in these times of frenetic entertainment and ever increasing decibels operatic and dramatic societies still seem to be flourishing, and that the operas of Gilbert and Sullivan main-tain their place in audiences' affection.

Long may they last!

Cynthia Morey

Oxfordshire 2006

To John and Nick
who know all about these things!

A WORLD THAT'S ALL OUR OWN

CHAPTER I

An air of expectancy reigned in Sandra Ogilvie's sitting room. Perfectly choreographed flames from the imitation log fire cast a flickering light over the awaiting chairs. A well-polished upright piano gleamed in one corner, and an illuminated cocktail cabinet made a gentle contribution to the scene, enhanced by the glow from a couple of strategically placed table lamps. For a discreet and flattering lighting plot, Blanche Dubois herself could have done no better. On the wall, on the piano, on each small table, on every available horizontal surface were elaborately framed photographs; Sandra as Yum-Yum in 'The Mikado', as Maria in 'The Dancing Years', as Josephine in 'HMS Pinafore', as Laurey in 'Oklahoma', as Eliza in 'My Fair Lady'. . . . .

The winning smile, the graceful pose, the knowing glance, the tragic gesture- each photograph portrayed Sandra starring in a Marleigh Operatic Society production. The room was almost a shrine.

Enter Sandra herself. The carefully planned lighting made it difficult to assess her age, which was in fact just over fifty. She was of medium height and inclined to plumpness, which, kept determinedly in check, was not unattractive. Her hair, an artificial but subtle blond, was styled to frame her face in a youthful manner. Skilful make-up kept the years at bay to a certain extent, and it was only in a harsher light that the lines under her eyes and at the corner of her mouth were visible. Sandra was clever with her clothes, too. The soft rose cashmere sweater she wore not only flattered her complexion, but disguised the slightly spreading waist line against which she battled in vain. Sandra crossed the room to check her appearance in the mirror above the fireplace. Patting her hair complacently, she hummed a snatch from 'The Desert Song', Marleigh's last production, in which, of course, she had played the leading role of Margot. Tonight was, for her, one of the most important dates in the calendar. The operatic society committee was to assemble at seven o'clock to decide on the next production. This accomplished, life for Sandra would once more take on a new and delightful meaning.

The sound of the doorbell interrupted her pleasant thoughts, and a slight frown of annoyance furrowed her brow as she glanced at the clock. It was only six-fifty- someone was early. 'It's sure to be Doreen,' she thought. And it was. Opening the front door, Sandra smiled sweetly at the somewhat dishevelled figure standing on the step.

'Oh, you *are* punctual, Doreen!' she said, with a touch of sarcasm completely wasted on the newcomer, 'Do come in.'

Doreen strode into the hall, clutching a mass of bulging files, papers, and a sagging plastic bag.

'Goodness, it must be blowing a gale,' said Sandra, surveying the first arrival with disapproval, 'Would you like to tidy up before the others arrive?'

'Oh- d'you think I need to? Suppose I'd better,' said Doreen, 'Came on my bike, of course- always like to do my bit for the environment-'

'Let me take your coat,' Sandra intervened hastily, fearing an ecological discourse. 'You know where the cloakroom is- just along the hall.' Doreen dumped her files on a chair, turned to go, then remembered her plastic bag.

'Oh- made these this afternoon when I got back from school.'

'What are they, dear?' enquired Sandra, peering doubtfully into the bag.

'Just a few fairy cakes,' replied Doreen cheerfully, 'So kind of you and Fred to entertain us mob every year,' and she breezed out of the room.

'*Fairy* cakes?' muttered Sandra, 'They weigh a ton.'

Doreen Clegg was a maths teacher at the local comprehensive, and though she grumbled about all the hard work involved, she actually enjoyed it, and adored the young people she taught. To describe her as plain would be an understatement. She peered at the world through thick glasses, and her haphazard clothes did nothing to enhance her appearance. They must surely have been hastily bought at various charity shops with no thought at all as to style or colour. Doreen's hair, greying and wiry, defied all efforts to restrain it- if indeed there were any. As she did nothing to it except wash it and have it cut when she thought of it, its unruly state was not surprising. But in spite of all these visual disadvantages, most of her pupils had a soft spot for 'old Cleggie'. And she could certainly teach.

Sandra carried Doreen's offering into her immaculate kitchen, where a laden trolley awaited the culmination of tonight's deliberations. Everything was tastefully arranged and looked delicious, and Sandra wondered how she could dispose of the unwanted fairy cakes without causing offence.

Arranging them on a small plate, she selected an unobtrusive place on the lower shelf, hoping they might be overlooked without Doreen noticing. After all, she reasoned, they didn't really go with smoked salmon sandwiches and black forest gateau.

The doorbell rang again. 'Fred! Fred! What on earth are you doing?' shouted Sandra in tones guaranteed to reach the back of the upper circle at Drury Lane. 'People are arriving!'

 Footsteps padded down the stairs. 'OK, love- I'll get it!' came a reassuring voice, as Sandra's husband Fred hurried to obey orders. They had been married for nearly thirty years, and though the marriage had sadly been childless, Fred was as besotted with his wife as he had been on their wedding day, supporting her operatic performances with wholehearted enthusiasm. No first- or last- night went by without an enormous bouquet for Sandra. He had been treasurer of the society for many years, his work as manager of the local branch of a national building society fitting him admirably for the post. Fred watched Sandra's every performance, sitting or standing if the house was full, unable to take his eyes off her. Tonight he was almost as excited as his wife to know what the next show would be, and which leading role she would play. A kindly, comfortable man in his late fifties, Fred was balding and slightly plump, with a sudden smile that lit up his rather homely face and gave a fleeting glimpse of the attractive young man with whom Sandra had fallen in love so many years ago.

Voices in the hall proclaimed the arrival of Eileen and Desmond Partridge, chairwoman and stage manager respectively. It was difficult to imagine how these two had originally got together. Eileen, though matronly in figure, was rather genteel, and spoke in pleasantly modulated tones. Desmond, by contrast, was loud and rather brash, with a tendency to laugh loudly and irritatingly at his own jokes. These were usually somewhat crude in nature and often elicited surreptitious reprimands from his disapproving wife.

Fred ushered Eileen and Desmond into the sitting room. Sandra hurried in from the kitchen with a cheerful greeting, and the two women exchanged an affectionate kiss.

'Hello, Eileen, you do look well,' exclaimed Sandra.

'So do you. How was the cruise?' asked Eileen.

'Oh- lovely! Fred and I simply adore our fortnight in the sun every February,' enthused Sandra. 'We come back fighting fit for the next show, don't we, Fred?' Fred nodded fondly. 'I feel ten years younger.'

'And you look it, dear,' said Eileen warmly, then suddenly realised that her remark was slightly unfortunate. 'Not that you needed to, of course,' she added hurriedly.

Sandra pretended not to hear Eileen's remark. 'Now, do sit down,' she said .'Terry, Norma and George will be here any minute. Doreen's already arrived. Jack can't come tonight, because he's conducting 'HMS Pinafore' over at Edgley. It's their last night. Did you see it?'

'Yes,' said Eileen, 'Their principals weren't bad, but I couldn't help remembering you as Josephine, Sandra. The way you sang that song in the second act- those wonderful high notes-' Sandra smiled modestly. 'And of course, you're such an actress. . . . But the chorus were quite good, and Jack conducted beautifully, as he always does. Such bright tempos- I can't bear Gilbert and Sullivan dragged along- it loses all its sparkle.'

'It doesn't seem a year since the meeting to discuss our last production, does it?' said Fred heartily. The years fly by, don't they, love?'

This observation received a sour look from Sandra, for the passage of time was something about which she was not keen to be reminded. Luckily, before the subject could be pursued, Doreen arrived back from her 'tidying up' session, which, seemingly, had not had the slightest effect on her appearance.

'Hello, all!' she greeted everyone enthusiastically, 'Hasn't it seemed ages since our last show? I must say I do miss the Operatic during the 'off' season- how about doing two productions a year, eh?'

Doreen's rash suggestion produced expressions of good-humoured horror and protest from the assembled company.

I was only joking.' she continued, 'Don't suppose I'd really have time. School takes up such a lot of my so-called leisure hours. Been an awful day today- double maths period with Four Beta-ugh!' There were murmurs of sympathy, though everyone knew that a double maths period for Doreen was probably one of the highlights of her week.

'Sit down, love,' said Fred, 'Take the weight off your feet.'

'I'll sit on this pouffe,' said Doreen, 'It looks nice and comfy.'

'Which reminds me,' said Desmond, 'Where's Terry?'

'Desmond!' hissed Eileen reprovingly. 'Now- has anyone got any ideas for the next show? We didn't do quite so well as usual with 'Desert Song', did we, Fred?'

Fred shuffled some papers and ran his eye down a column of figures. 'Er-no. . . . But the bar takings were up considerably,' he added, on a more cheerful note.

Desmond gave one of his raucous laughs. "I expect they all needed a stiff one before facing Act II-'

Sandra broke in defensively, 'You can't please everyone all the time. And Boddington Operatic did 'Desert Song' a couple of years back. We should have paid more attention to that-'

'Yes. . . . I know they did,' reflected Eileen. 'But our production was far superior to theirs, so much more professional. That gorgeous backcloth with the pyramids- didn't Alf light them beautifully?'

'A pity they used to wave about every time anyone went across the back to the bloody gents,' said Desmond, 'Sort of spoilt the illusion.'

'Desmond!' said Eileen despairingly. 'But wasn't Ron Catesby super as the Red Shadow?' she enthused. 'Absolutely stole the show-' She realised rather too late what she had said, and received a frigid look from Sandra. 'As far as the men were concerned, of course,' she added hurriedly .

'Oh, well- everyone to their own taste,' said Sandra coldly. Personally, I always think he sings slightly flat. And I wish he wouldn't eat garlic on the day of the performance, especially when he knows very well there are intimate love duets.'

The sound of the doorbell prevented any further revelations about Ron's personal habits, and Fred went to usher in Norma and George Phillips.

'Norma, how lovely to see you- there's a comfortable chair over there- and George, look- there's room on the sofa next to Desmond- that's right.' Sandra bustled about, getting her guests settled, while Fred disposed of their coats.

George, a solid, dependable sort, looked after publicity, and supervised the box office, programmes and posters. He ran a small printing firm in Marleigh and was thus able to save quite a bit of money for the society where these things were concerned. Very tall and broad, he was a complete contrast to his diminutive wife, Norma. She was wardrobe mistress, a duty she executed with great efficiency, and, when called for, a considerable amount of ingenuity. There was much chat and laughter when they arrived, and soon everyone was seated and ready for the evening's important proceedings.

'Coffee, anyone?' enquired Sandra, 'Or ought we to get down to business? Terry's still to come, of course- said he might be a little delayed- but we could still do some preliminaries.'

'Oh, let's begin,' said Norma. 'Coffee will be lovely later.' Eileen sat up straighter at this suggestion, and prepared to take the chair.

'Well, everyone, our main purpose here tonight is to choose our next production. I'm sure you all have your own ideas about this- I've made a short list of possibilities myself, and I expect you've done the same.'

'We certainly have,' said Sandra. 'This year we must make sure that we do a show which is really 'box office' and hasn't been done anywhere in the area for ages. For instance, no-one's put on 'The Merry Widow' or 'Die Fledermaus' for years.'

'Die what?' muttered Desmond, only to be suppressed quickly by Eileen.

'Well, 'Gay Rosalinda', if you prefer-' Sandra started to explain. '

'Oh no, let's keep it heterosexual!' said Desmond.

'Do be quiet, Desmond!' said Eileen with a sigh.

'That's the version usually performed by amateur societies,' finished Sandra.

Fred stroked his chin thoughtfully. 'The Merry Widow,' he mused. 'Yes- you'd make a lovely Widow, Sandra. It's one of the more mature roles-'

Fred found himself on the receiving end of one of Sandra's 'looks' at this remark, and hastily went on, 'And it's got class. All those gorgeous tunes-'

'And beautiful frocks!' squeaked Norma, her voice rising an octave with excitement.

George looked doubtful. 'Yes, but is it box office?' he pondered.

If you ask me, it's time we did another Gilbert and Sullivan. Now, we haven't done 'The Mikado' since- let me see- 1980. That's always popular.'

Putting on his glasses, George got up to examine one of the photographs on the piano.

'Oh, you were a lovely Yum-Yum, Sandra! My, that takes me back- 1980- it doesn't seem possible-'

'I can't think it was as long ago as that,' said Sandra shortly.

'Oh, it *was*, dear!' insisted Norma. 'I remember because I was expecting Tracy. I had morning sickness every evening of performance week, and she'll be twenty-two in May. And the same week our next door neighbour had her third caesarian,' persisted Norma.

'Her *third*?' exclaimed Eileen with great interest, 'I didn't know you could *have* three-'

'Why didn't they just put a zip in?' suggested Desmond, only to receive another exasperated look from his wife.

Sandra was not too keen to hear any more gynaecological reminiscences, especially when they spanned so many years.

'Well, anyway,' she intervened, 'Who's got some more suggestions?'

Doreen cleared her throat nervously. 'I think it's time to change our policy,' she announced.

'Whatever do you mean, Doreen?' George asked.

Doreen sat on the edge of her seat, and took a deep breath.

'Don't you think it's about time we thought about trying to attract a *younger* audience? And cast, for that matter,' she added daringly, studiously avoiding Sandra's hostile gaze.

'Go on, Doreen,' said Eileen quietly.

'How about doing something like 'Grease', for instance? Or we could try 'West Side Story'- that's not so new now, of course, but it would certainly attract some younger blood-'

Sandra was outraged. 'Of course, if you want to lose all your *experienced* performers-'

Doreen realised she was now in deep water, but she pressed on manfully.

'I know that, with one or two exceptions, we've always tended to stick to the same cast, but I believe the time has come to change our tactics. After all, where is the society of the future coming from if we don't let the young ones in now?'

Doreen looked round the assembled committee, but no-one met her eyes.

There was an awkward silence, broken only by Desmond clearing his throat, and an audible sniff from Sandra. The doorbell rang, sounding, in the circumstances, unusually loud.

'That'll be Terry,' said Fred with relief. 'He can advise us.' And he hurried to the front door to admit the last committee member, glad to escape the uncomfortable atmosphere for a moment.

Terry Althorpe entered the room with a flourish. Dressed flamboyantly, he took centre stage, as always, and assumed a theatrical pose. He wore his hair rather long, and its natural colour was enhanced by subtle highlights. This was easy for him to achieve, as he was proprietor and head stylist of a rather chic ladies' hairdressing salon. Terry had very briefly 'trodden the boards' himself, having once years ago, done an obscure tour of Oklahoma. No theatrical managements had rushed to secure his talents after this, so hairdressing had seemed to offer a viable alternative. Starting as a junior, Terry had worked his way up to his present exalted position, a process which would have been most unlikely in the theatre. But he made sure that everyone was aware of his stage experience, and because of this had been approached by Marleigh several years previously to direct their annual productions. He revelled in this, and did a very good job, indulging his own unfulfilled stage ambitions at the same time.

Terry sensed the atmosphere immediately he entered the room. All, he quickly deduced, was not well with the committee. He decided to jump in with both feet.

'Hi, folks!' he greeted them. 'Sorry to be late- my last client kept me *ages!* Well, have you chosen our next show? What's it to be- 'West Side Story', eh?' Terry was not prepared for the embarrassed silence which met his ill chosen words. He looked around, puzzled. Finally Sandra broke the silence.

'You'll never believe it, Terry, but Doreen actually *has* proposed West Side Story. We couldn't possibly cast it- there's nothing any of our principals could play. I could always help Norma in the wardrobe, I suppose. . . .or sell programmes. . . .' and Sandra tailed off into an angry silence.

'Now, now, now-' soothed Terry, 'I'm sure there are lots of other ideas. Quite honestly, Doreen, could you really see old Cyril Higgins or Arthur Dobbs as Jets and Sharks in 'West Side'? It's just not their scene- we have to bear that in mind-'

'But don't you see, that's the whole *point*!' interrupted Doreen vehemently. We need *younger* acting members- this society must be progressive. No audience will come year after year to see the same old shows, the same old faces-' At these words Doreen realised she had gone too far- 'However good they are!' she finished desperately.

'Well- I must say-' Sandra was, for once, lost for words.

'But Doreen,' reasoned Terry, 'We've got quite a lot of young folk. Look at Sharon Ackroyd and Angie Greenwood- they're in their early twenties. Oh, and Lisa Preston- now, she's a pretty lass-'

'Yes, and that's only her face,' said Desmond, 'You should see her-'

'Not now, Desmond!' warned Eileen.

'And what about Ian Richardson and David Waterhouse, among the chaps,' put in George.

'Kevin Cartwright, too- and there are several others under forty-' added Fred.

'Under *forty*?' said Doreen angrily. 'We need some under twenty-five!'

'Well, we *have* got some young members,' insisted Norma.

Doreen sighed. 'Yes, I know,' she allowed, 'They're in the society now, but for how much longer? They never get any farther than the chorus, or bit parts-'

Eileen made an attempt to remonstrate, but Doreen was unstoppable.

'We have auditions, yes- but the outcome's a foregone conclusion!'

'I'm sure the audition panel is very fair,' said Sandra firmly. 'We always have a couple of impartial adjudicators from outside the society.'

Doreen was determined to stick to her guns. 'All the same-' she began.

Fred broke in firmly, 'We *need* experienced principals. We may be amateurs, but folk pay good money to see the show.'

'Sometimes a pretty face and a fresh young voice make up for a lack of stagecraft,' Doreen went on, 'That would come with experience- if they were allowed to acquire any!'

Eileen decided that, as chair, it was time to intervene.

'Well, whatever opinion we may all have about that, we must get down to the job of selecting our next production. Here, for what it's worth, is my own suggestion list: 'White Horse Inn', 'The Student Prince', 'The Pirates of Penzance', and 'Merrie England'- not necessarily in that order.'

There were murmurs of appreciation at Eileen's selection. Doreen could not restrain herself.

'But they're all so stuffy, so old-fashioned- has-beens!'

A hostile silence followed this outburst, broken at last by Eileen, who spoke with great dignity.

'Those are my suggestions. Sandra- ideas from you?'

'Well, at the risk of being called a 'has-been',' replied Sandra pointedly, 'My list is as follows: as previously mentioned, 'Die Fledermaus' and 'The Merry Widow' are two of my favourites, then 'The Land of Smiles' (also by Franz Lehar), and 'Countess

Maritza'. Real operetta, to be sung by trained voices and acted by a mature and experienced cast. This is, after all, an *operatic* society. That's all.'

Noises of approval greeted Sandra's comments.

'Thank you, Sandra,' said Eileen. 'Fred?'

'Sandra's got something there,' replied Fred, predictably. 'Those are first rate shows- spectacular, too. Audiences want that these days- something colourful to look at.'

'Ye-es. . . . said George, doubtfully, 'But are they 'box office'? My money's still on 'The Mikado'- or what was that other one on your list, Eileen?'

'The other G&S?' said Eileen, 'Oh, you mean 'The Pirates of Penzance'.'

'Yes, 'Pirates'!' replied George enthusiastically. 'We could update 'Pirates', Doreen, if you're after something a bit more daring-'

'Yes, how about doing it topless?' said Desmond, rubbing his hands at the idea. 'Just think of those girls jumping over the rocks-'

'That's enough, Desmond!' Eileen glared at her husband.

George was deep in thought.

'Now,' he continued, his mind on box office receipts, 'you'd have a big attraction there- quality stuff, popular, colourful, and easy-to-hire costumes and sets.'

'That's a point, George,' said Eileen, making notes. 'How about you, Desmond?'

'Yes, all joking apart, I'm keen on 'Pirates', too- lovely music, for principals and chorus. It's time we did another Gilbert and Sullivan- gets bums on seats! The audience love 'em!' Desmond snatched up a sheaf of paper, rolled it up and held it to his lips. 'Taran-tara. taran-tara!' he sang raucously, in a crude imitation of the Policemen's Chorus.

'Thank you, Desmond,' said Eileen hurriedly. 'Terry?'

'The Pirates of Penzance'. . . . . .' mused Terry. 'Yes- I must say

I'd be happy to do that- or any other G&S for that matter- we've rather neglected them of late. Other than that, I've always wanted to do 'The Arcadians'. The music's wonderful, but the book wants updating, and it's an expensive show to put on. No, all in all, I think it ought to be 'Pirates.'

'Right, Terry,' said Eileen, making a note of Terry's choice.

'D'you know, we haven't done 'Pirates' since- let me see- seventy-eight,' said George, consulting his list. 'It's high time it had an airing. Yes, I'll settle for 'Pirates'.'

'God, those policemen always bring the house down!' laughed Desmond. 'Hey, Sandra, don't you remember, you stood there as Mabel and said, 'Sergeant, approach' and little Archie Hancock got his truncheon stuck between the Sergeant's legs- the whole lot of 'em went down like a pack of cards! Got a standing ovation! Now, that's show business, that is!'

There was laughter from everyone at this, except Doreen, who sat staring down at the papers on her lap.

'Have you any interesting ideas, Norma?' asked Eileen, when the laughter had died down.

Norma sat on the edge of her chair with her head on one side, rather like some small bird, while she carefully considered.

'Well, of course,' she said finally, 'as wardrobe mistress, the costumes are my prime concern, so I'm in favour of a show with lovely dresses- our lives are drab enough these days, goodness knows. Of course, it must have good tunes, too. Ye-es. .. Pirates would be nice. . . You can have crinolines or bustles ... Even the older ladies look nice in those-'

'You realise they're all supposed to be General Stanley's *daughters*, I suppose,' remarked Doreen tartly. He'd have to be about eighty-seven to be the father of Gladys Parker or Vera Pemberton- not to mention quite a few others-'

'But there's such a thing as stage licence, Doreen!' said Norma earnestly.' And it's amazing how young some of those older ladies look when they're made up, and nicely lit-'

'We oughtn't to *need* stage licence!' said Doreen angrily. 'There are enough genuinely young folk around if only they were given the incentive!'

She would have gone on in this way, but Eileen intervened firmly.

'Thank you, Doreen, you've made your point. Gladys and Vera have been in Marleigh Operatic for over thirty years, and they're not going to be turned out for any feckless youngsters who don't show up at half the rehearsals, or let everyone down just before performance week. People like them are the backbone of the society. If you've any constructive ideas to add to this discussion, we'd be glad to hear them. Otherwise.....' Doreen stood up. She struggled to control her feelings.

'Then I'm afraid I can't continue any longer as secretary,' she announced with deep emotion. 'You're all set on the old pot-boilers, the same old cast, the ageing chorus. You won't be moved, you won't look into the future! You want to go on living in the past, indulging yourselves in your annual week of glory. Well, I can't be part of it any more.' Doreen bundled all her files together and handed them to Eileen.

'Here are all the society papers. You'll find them in good order. I'll send in my resignation officially, of course. I wish you success.'

Everyone watched in disbelief as she walked out of the room, head held high, obviously on the verge of tears. Eileen got up as if to follow, but Fred motioned to her to remain seated.

'I'll get her coat and see her out,' he said in a low voice. I think we should just let her go. She'll simmer down and maybe see things differently tomorrow. She's too overwrought to reason with tonight.'

CHAPTER 2

Nobody spoke as Fred left the room. Voices were heard in the hall, Fred's conciliatory, Doreen's monosyllabic. The front door opened and closed, and Fred returned, sighing deeply and shaking his head.

'Well! exclaimed Sandra.

'What a carry-on! I wonder what's eating her?' said George.

'What she needs is a man,' said Desmond. 'She wants a good-'

'I think we can conclude our business,' Eileen broke in hastily. 'We'll take a vote, shall we? 'The Pirates of Penzance' is the most likely choice, it seems. Let's have a show of hands.'

Everyone raised their hand except Sandra, who seemed strangely reluctant, and Fred, who was watching her closely to see what she would do. She looked around, shrugged her shoulders, and rather hesitantly raised her hand, whereupon Fred immediately followed suit.

Eileen looked relieved. 'Well, 'Pirates' it is! Good. We can announce our decision to the members on Tuesday, order scores and libretti, and arrange audition pieces. Terry, you'll set the dialogue, won't you?'

'Yes, of course,' replied Terry, 'I've got an old libretto at home somewhere.'

'Well, that's all right, then. Jack will decide on the vocal pieces as usual. He's sorry not to be with us tonight, but I do know that he will approve our decision. I purposely did not mention this till now in case it influenced anyone's choice, but when I showed him my list yesterday he said that he'd be very keen to do 'Pirates'.'

General pleasure was expressed at this satisfactory conclusion to the meeting.

Coffee, everyone?' enquired Sandra brightly. 'Won't be a minute- give me a hand, Fred.'

As Sandra and Fred went to attend to the refreshments, everyone relaxed, and the atmosphere became less formal. Terry stretched luxuriously, and gave a long sigh of relief.

'Wonderful!' he said, 'that's settled for another year. And apart from Doreen we were unanimous in our decision.'

'Somehow I got the idea that Sandra wasn't very pleased,' remarked Eileen thoughtfully.

'Oh, I expect she was concerned about Doreen,' said Terry. 'It was rather an unpleasant interlude.'

'Pity about her,' said Desmond. 'She's a damn good secretary- it won't be easy to replace her. D'you think she'll come round?'

George nodded slowly.

'Oh, I expect so. She lives alone- got nothing much in her life except her teaching. Dotes on the operatic society. She can be a bit excitable sometimes, especially when she gets a bee in her bonnet.'

'It's that comprehensive school,' squeaked Norma indignantly. 'She was never like that when she taught at Marleigh Grammar.'

Eileen consulted her list of society members thoughtfully.

'We can certainly cast 'Pirates' easily. The part of Mabel is usually the stumbling block for amateur societies. That song is every soprano's Waterloo- it's so high, and all that florid coloratura-whatever the audition panel may think about age and appearance, there's only Sandra with those glorious high notes- especially that top Db. Unless you've got that, you can't sing Mabel.'

Norma clasped her hands in joyful anticipation.

'And Ron Catesby'll sing Frederic like a dream- that gorgeous song in Act-'

'Ye-es. . . ' interrupted George, 'he'd sing it OK, but he'd have a bit of a job convincing the audience he's twenty-one. He can get away with most leading roles, but don't forget that in Pirates Frederic's age is part of the plot. There are constant references to the fact that he's twenty-one all through the show.'

'Well, if Ron doesn't do it, I don't know who else,' said Norma.

'There's that Scottish chap,' suggested George, 'Hamish Macrae-now, he's got a good voice-'

Eileen shook her head. 'He's got such a broad accent.'

Desmond guffawed. 'It'd have to be called 'The Pirates of Aberdeen' or something!' he roared.

'Oh, don't be silly, Desmond,' said Eileen, with a sigh of resignation.

'Terry looked doubtful. 'He's not terribly romantic looking,' he said thoughtfully. 'I think it's those teeth.'

'And that limp doesn't help,' added Eileen.

'But you know, he does disguise it terribly well on stage,' said Norma earnestly. 'I remember when he danced the Cachucha in 'The Gondoliers' over at Edgley a couple of years ago, you hardly noticed.'

Terry ran his fingers through his well-tended locks, deep in concentration.

'Of course, there's Ian Richardson,' he said at last.

'Too inexperienced.' Eileen dismissed the suggestion decisively.

'His voice is good, though,' persisted Terry. 'And he's a good-looking lad- with a bit of coaching. . . . .'

Desmond winked. 'Private lessons, eh, Terry!'

Terry took this with good humour. 'If only!' he laughed.

'Anyway, it's no good conjecturing- the audition panel will decide,' declared George. 'Who have we got this year- the usual adjudicators, I suppose?'

'Well, there's Jack, Terry and myself, of course,' replied Eileen, 'and from outside we have Hilary Armitage and Jonathan Wilkes. As you know, Hilary teaches drama, so will advise on the acting side, and Mr Wilkes, who's new to us, is head of the music department at Framley Hal1.'

'He teaches singing, doesn't he?' asked Norma.

'Yes. He'll be invaluable from that angle. It's essential to have a couple of impartial judges on the panel- looks good,' said Eileen.

Framley Hall was a prestigious private school a few miles from Marleigh, particularly noted for musical achievement, and there were nods of approval at Jonathan Wilkes' inclusion on the panel.

With a welcome rattle of china, Fred appeared with the trolley, Sandra following behind with a large percolator. The scent of freshly-brewed coffee filled the air. Having handed out plates and paper napkins, Fred was just about to produce Doreen's battered rock cakes from the lower tray. Sandra had forgotten to dispose of them after Doreen's dramatic departure, and she now hastened to whisk them away from Fred to a safe place behind one of her larger portraits. Puzzled, Fred handed round the smoked salmon sandwiches instead.

'What are we going to do about scenery this year?' enquired Desmond, reaching out for a second sandwich before anyone else was halfway through their first.

'Wouldn't it be absolutely wonderful if we could design our own?' said Terry, fired with imagination. 'I can just visualise an entirely new conception of that old rocky shore- ethereal. . . misty. . . shimmering. . . .'

Sandra was more down to earth. 'What we'll actually get is that tired old royal blue backcloth with an improbable pirate ship sitting there completely motionless in a turbulent sea-'

'With creases all across the sky, that you simply can't get out,' laughed Norma.

'And those awful canvas-covered rocks that shake about when the girls clamber down!' added Eileen. 'I remember Gladys put her foot through one once- she was completely trapped, and had to sing the whole of the opening chorus rooted to the spot.'

Everyone roared with laughter at this, then Terry intervened. 'You don't think it might be possible to build our own scenery? There are some handy lads in the society, and I think I might be able to design it-'

'We'd probably have a mauve sky if you did,' said Desmond, but George took the suggestion more seriously.

'It would be nice if we could,' he said. 'But what would we do with it afterwards? We've no storage, and that would be an added expense. It's a pity, but.. . .'

'Well, at least we could try a different hire firm,' suggested Sandra. 'I had good reports of one in Birmingham the other day. I made a note of it in my diary.' She flicked through the pages. 'Yes, here it is- 'Easy Stages' it's called. Then there's another just north of Oxford- 'Scene Stealers' we could try both of those.'

'Good,' said Eileen. 'Let's do that. Give me their addresses- oh, dear- that's Doreen's job. I do hope we can persuade her to withdraw her resignation.'

'Oh, I'm sure we can,' said Fred. 'She'll see things differently tomorrow.'

'This gateau is simply gorgeous,' said Norma. 'You didn't make it, did you?'

''Fraid not,' laughed Sandra. 'It's courtesy of Monsieur Sainsbury! Do have some more,' and she placed another generous slice on Norma's plate, ignoring her half- hearted protestations. 'You don't have to worry about your figure, you never put on an ounce.'

Norma giggled. She knew this was true, for in spite of her weakness for pastries and chocolates, her diminutive figure showed no sign of her self indulgence.

'I've been thinking,' said Terry suddenly. 'Remember George said we could update 'Pirates'?'

'Oh, I was only joking.' George sounded worried.

'But we *could*-' persisted Terry, his imagination working overtime.

'Do it topless, d'you mean?' suggested Desmond, with a lascivious gesture. 'Good-oh!'

'Be quiet, Desmond!' Eileen glared at her husband. 'What have you got in mind, Terry?'

Terry placed his cup and saucer carefully on the trolley. 'Well-what do you say to a nineteen-twenties version? It would be such fun! Just think of all those girls as flappers- 'Won't you Charleston with me?' Terry sang, standing up and executing a few nifty steps in the middle of the room. He clasped his hands in delight. 'Oh, I can see it *all!*'

Everyone was silent as they contemplated this revolutionary idea. Norma was the first to speak. Her disappointment was obvious.

'No crinolines or bustles?' she mourned. 'And how will some of the larger ladies look in short skirts?'

Terry contemplated this problem. 'I think if we do a twenties version,' he said slowly, 'We'll have to audition the ladies' chorus-'

'And their legs, if the skirts are going to be short,' gloated Desmond. 'I could help with that-'

'No, you couldn't, Desmond,' snapped Eileen crossly. She looked worried. 'The ladies aren't going to like auditioning,' she said.

'I'm afraid they'll have to, Eileen,' replied Terry.

'But what about the older ones?' she persisted. 'What will you do about them?'

'Well. . . actually, Doreen was right on one count,' he admitted. 'If they're supposed to be the Major General's daughters, they shouldn't actually be *older* than him. . . . but, don't worry about that, they won't be left out- you'll see.'

'It's an exciting idea,' decided Fred. 'Lots of societies update productions, but Marleigh's always been very traditional- people expect it of us. It'll be such a surprise for everyone. I'm all for it.'

Gradually everyone was coming round to the proposed innovation, even Norma.

'Of course, nineteen-twenties dresses can be quite pretty,' she admitted. 'Flying panels, handkerchief points, nice pastel shades. . . . . Oh- but what about the men?'

'Now, let me see. . . ' mused Terry. 'The policemen are just policemen, so as long as we stipulate the period, the costume people should be able to cope with that. But the pirates. . . I know! The script says they are all 'noblemen who have gone wrong', so how about a sprinkling of old school ties and blazers- striped if possible- mixed up with the usual piratical gear?'

'Brilliant!' enthused George. 'And how about a pith helmet- old Benson has one. I know-'

'And a top hat or two, perhaps,' added Fred, catching the mounting enthusiasm.

'We *must* have a few boaters, of course,' said Eileen.

'One of 'em could have a battered coronet!' suggested Desmond.

Terry threw up his hands in ecstasy. 'Gorgeous ideas-we'll do it! we'll do it!'

'Now,' pronounced George gravely, 'I think we must keep this quiet. Let people know we're going to do 'Pirates', of course- that goes without saying- even that it's going to be a different sort of production, but that's all. Lets keep it under our hats and give everyone a big surprise- particularly the Boddington folk. They always turn up on the first night- this time they won't know what's hit 'em!'

There was enthusiastic agreement on this point, for Boddington was a rival society, and competition between the two of them was always fierce.

'Any other business tonight?' said Eileen, gathering up her papers. She looked at her watch. 'Heavens- is that the time- I'd no idea. It's been a splendid meeting- apart from the drama with Doreen, of course. But I'm sure that can be sorted out.'

But what shall we do about her?' said Norma anxiously. "We need a secretary, and we need one now. Getting a production underway involves a lot of work.'

'Perhaps I'd better have a word with her tomorrow,' decided Eileen. 'When she hears that we're going to audition the ladies' chorus and update the show, she may come round.'

'Oh, she *must*!' said Terry. 'It's going to be quite marvellous!'

'That seems to be it, then,' said Norma. 'Come along. George- we really must go.' She turned to Sandra and Fred. 'Thank you, both, for your hospitality. It's been a stimulating evening, one way and another.'

There was a general collecting up of pens, papers and files as everyone prepared to leave, and Fred went into the hall to fetch coats. Terry, on his way to help, stopped to look at some of Sandra's pictures.

'I adore all these photographs of past shows,' he said. 'What a lot you've done, Sandra! Ooh- just look at that one- what is it?'

'Oh, that was The 'Maid of the Mountains'- it was a lovely production,' replied Sandra.

'Goodness,' exclaimed Terry. 'Whenever did the society do *that*?'

Sandra looked a little nonplussed. 'Well... er . . . a few years ago,' she answered vaguely. 'Here's Fred with your coat, Terry,' she added hastily, anxious not to have to go into further chronological details. It had indeed been a very long time ago, for 'The Maid of the Mountains' had been Sandra's very first show with Marleigh Operatic Society.

'Wrap up warmly, all of you,' advised Fred. 'It's cold out.'

There was a chorus of goodbyes and thank-yous and 'see you next Tuesday' as the committee filed out into the street. Finally Fred closed the front door and followed his wife back into the sitting room.

'Well,' he smiled happily, 'that was most satisfactory, in spite of the little contretemps with Doreen. Still, I expect she'll come round. Are you pleased with the decision, love?'

'Not particularly,' was Sandra's response.

'Whatever do you mean?' Fred's forehead was puckered with concern. You voted for 'Pirates'- why did you, if you didn't want to do it?'

'Because everyone else was unanimous. What difference would it have made if I- and you, for that matter- had opposed it? We would have been in the minority- we'd have been overruled.'

'But you're our leading lady, Sandra-' Fred was much troubled by his wife's attitude.

'And we've just chosen the one show that'll catch me out,' replied Sandra bitterly. 'That song- 'Poor Wand'ring One'- I don't think I can sing it any more. I still have high notes, yes, but not those you need for Mabel. Or the vocal agility required for those coloratura runs and staccato passages. Oh, no, Fred- Mabel's the one role I'm afraid I can no longer sing.' Sandra struggled to hold back her tears.

'Not *sing* it? Of course you can sing it! No-one else can, that's for sure. Look how you did it last time-'

'That was *years* ago, Fred,' she said sadly. 'Years and years. . . .'

Fred put a comforting arm round her shoulders. 'Come on, now, love- you'll make a lovely Mabel, I know you will.'

Sandra sniffed. 'We'll see, Fred, we'll see,' she said dully.

'That's my girl.' Fred beamed, reassured that Sandra's self-doubt was just a temporary thing. 'Now, I'll just clear away the debris.' And, collecting up various cups and plates, Fred wheeled the trolley into the kitchen, whistling cheerfully. Of course Sandra could do it. She always did.

Left alone, Sandra wandered listlessly round the room until she came to a photograph of herself as Mabel in 'The Pirates of Penzance', so long ago. She gazed at it for a few seconds. The smooth young face looked back at her.

Sandra took the photograph from its place and put it in a drawer.

CHAPTER 3

The hall was filling up fast and most of the seats were already taken. Desmond was setting out more chairs as members of Marleigh Operatic Society assembled to hear which production they were to be involved in next. Excitement was at a premium, and conjecture was rife.

'Hold on, Des-' shouted George across the babble of voices. 'I'll give you a hand with those chairs.'

'Thanks, George,' said Desmond, 'We're going to need them all tonight. It'll be a full house. Everyone's always keen to know what the next show's going to be.'

'Hello- here comes Doreen,' exclaimed George in surprise. 'Eileen talked her round, then?'

'Oh, yes, eventually. It took a bit of doing, but you know how good Eileen is at that sort of thing. When old Doreen heard that we were going to audition the chorus, pick the younger ones and update the production, she said she'd give it a go. Hi, Doreen!' Desmond called out as she approached. 'Are we glad to see *you*!'

'Good evening,' said Doreen. 'Well, when Eileen told me you'd decided to move with the times, I thought I'd see how things work out. I don't think for a moment we've gone far enough, but it's a start.'

'You know there's a small piece in the Herald this week saying we'd welcome new members, don't you?' said George. 'We thought perhaps some young folk might turn up.'

'It's to be hoped so,' Doreen replied, her eye on Gladys Parker and Vera Pemberton, who were just taking their seats, complete with knitting.

'Ah, there's Sandra' said Doreen, 'I must have a word with her,' and she made her way through the last few stragglers who were looking for seats.

'Oh, well,' said George, 'so long as she's happy-'

'Talk about young ones,' exclaimed Desmond excitedly, 'who's that dolly bird over there? What a gorgeous pair of-'

Eileen appeared at his side just in time to overhear his remark. 'Desmond!' she said accusingly.

'*Ear-rings*, I was going to say, if you'd only have let me finish,' replied her husband, with an injured air.

'That's as maybe,' said Eileen, unconvinced. 'You'd better come to the platform now. It's nearly time to begin, and there are a couple of things we need to clear up before the meeting starts.'

Comfortably seated in the second row, Gladys and Vera were getting their knitting out of capacious bags.

'What a pretty colour, Glad,' remarked Vera. 'What are you making?'

'Oh, it's for Kylie- that's my fourth grandchild,' said Gladys. 'It's a cardigan- rather a difficult pattern, but I've nearly got to a plain bit, so it'll be just the thing for the meeting. What d'you reckon the next show'll be?'

'I don't know, Glad. Wouldn't mind a Gilbert and Sullivan- they always go down well. And I know all the words and music- saves having to learn anything new.'

There was a pause, while Vera negotiated a complicated section of pattern.

'Glad,' she said seriously, 'I've been a bit worried. Suppose it's 'Iolanthe'? All the ladies' chorus are fairies! Well- I really don't see how we could be fairies any longer, do you? I mean- I know it's satire, but don't you think it would be carrying things a bit too far? Oh, damn! I've done a row of pearl instead of plain -'

'Whatever do you mean, Vera?' Gladys's eyes were wide with horror.' You surely don't mean give up the operatic? I couldn't- not after all these years-oh, no-'

'But, Glad,' said Vera doubtfully, 'What else could we do?'

'I do so look forward to these Tuesday nights. . . .the singing. . . . the company. . . the chat. .. Especially now Bert has gone. . . ' Gladys thought for a moment. 'I could get my hair touched up a

bit- and if we stood at the back where the lights aren't so bright.-
Oh, Vera- don't you think it'd be all right?'

But Vera was adamant. She had been thinking seriously for
some time about their future career in the operatic society, and
could see no other solution but to bow out gracefully sooner or
later, painful though it would be.

'We've got to face it, Glad. The day will come when we *have* to
step down. I reckon it could be here now. We'll see what show
the committee has chosen. But if it's one that needs a young chorus, well. . . . '

With that depressing prospect in view, both gave their attention
to their knitting. There was nothing more to be said.

Several of the younger women had gathered round the tall,
rather swaggering figure of Ron Catesby, who for many years
had played the leading tenor roles in the Marleigh productions.
It was difficult to guess Ron's exact age, though he was obviously
well into his middle years, for he was tall- a valuable asset for
a tenor- and well preserved. His hair, still fairly abundant, was
not allowed to display any grey, and had been tinted to a rather
unnatural brown. His slightly florid complexion and thicken-
ing waistline gave away the fact that youth had departed some
time ago. But Ron was a great character and looked very good
on stage, though his acting could be described as a bit 'ham'.
His great asset was his big natural tenor voice, which, though
rather undisciplined at times, never failed to thrill his audience.
His tendency to hang on to a top note as long as he could was a
source of constant annoyance to Sandra, who had been known
on occasion -to give him a sly dig, causing the sound to cease
abruptly. Ron was holding forth about his recent successes to the
admiring group. Ian Richardson, the hopeful young tenor who
had been mentioned during the committee meeting, strolled over
to hear what was going on.

'Hi, Ron! How's the voice?' he said, winking at one of the girls.

Ron cleared his throat in a high-pitched, tenor sort of way.

'Oh, pretty good, thanks Ian. Just done a week of 'Gondoliers'
over at Cranley Heath. Great success- stole all the notices, of

course, which didn't please the other principals much- but there you are. What's our next epic to be- have you heard?'

Ian shook his head. 'No idea. You'd have to employ Special Branch to get it out of our committee- though I did hear whispers of 'The Merry Widow' a few weeks ago.'

'Merry Widow', eh? Haven't had a go at that for years- suits me very well,' and Ron executed a few neat steps. 'I'm off to Chez Maxim' he warbled, to the amusement and admiration of his immediate audience, putting his arms round two of the girls, and swinging them into an exaggerated pose.

'I see there are one or two new faces here tonight,' continued Ron, 'She's attractive, over there- wonder if her singing's as good as her looks? Come on, girls, looks as if we're going to start- about time we found seats.' And Ron wandered off, followed by his admirers.

Ian was a good-looking young man- just the sort of material Doreen had in mind for leading roles, but with Ron Catesby firmly established in that capacity, it seemed that there was little chance for him. Fairly tall and slim, he had an easy charm which might have been a great asset on stage, had he been given an opportunity to display it. But he had to be content with the minor roles which usually came his way, and which he accepted cheerfully.

The girl Ron had spotted seemed to be by herself, and she was obviously wondering where to sit. Ian was not one to miss a chance.

'Hi, this your first time here? I think it's my duty to make new members feel at home. I'm Ian Richardson- tenor- rare species!' Ian received a warm smile from the newcomer.

'Sue Hebden- soprano- common species!' she responded. 'Yes, I'm new tonight, and I don't know a soul,' she admitted.

'Soon remedy that,' said Ian. 'Marleigh can do with some new talent- done anything like this before?'

'Not really,' said Sue. 'Did a bit at school- we had a good drama group- but that's past history. And I've had some singing lessons, that's all. It was my mother who saw the bit in the Herald, and persuaded me to come and see what goes on. She used to play the leads with the local society before we moved to Marleigh.'

'That sounds promising.' said Ian. 'D'you take after her? Have we got a new prima donna in our midst?'

Sue laughed. 'Shouldn't think so. I shall stay quietly in the background until I get to know everybody.'

'Oh, you must try for a part- we all do,' said Ian.

Sue shrugged her shoulders. 'We'll see,' she said, 'but I doubt it.'

There was a slight commotion at the door. Terry Althorpe appeared, dressed for the occasion in several shades of mauve. He stood still for a few seconds, to make sure that his arrival would not pass unnoticed.

'Good heavens, who's that?' asked Sue in amazement, 'talk about flamboyant! '

Ian laughed at her amazement. 'Oh, that's Terry Althorpe- he's our director of productions,' he said. 'He likes to look theatrical. Pale mauve's his favourite colour. I believe he actually was in 'the business' years ago- in some tour or other. But he didn't make it, and took up hairdressing instead. Never looked back- runs that posh salon in Marleigh High Street- you'll have seen it- 'Maison Terry'

'Oh, I know,' said Sue, 'the one with pale mauve blinds-'

'And the ladies of Marleigh come out with pale mauve hair to match,' laughed Ian. 'But, joking apart, Terry's a damn good producer- we could do a lot worse.'

Terry made his way to join the other committee members on the platform in a sort of royal progress, greeting various people effusively en route. The hubbub in the hall died down as Eileen rapped on the table for silence. Sue and Ian sat down in a couple of empty seats in the back row, and Desmond called out 'Quiet, everyone, please! Can we have a bit of hush?'

'Ladies and gentlemen- fellow members,' said Eileen, 'we have a great deal to talk about tonight. We have to inform you all of our current financial position following our last production, deal with some other business, and of course welcome new members, who we are delighted to see here this evening. But we know what you are all waiting to hear, and we don't propose to keep you in suspense. What is our next production to be? We have chosen 'The Pirates of Penzance.'

There were diverse reactions to this announcement: a ripple of applause, some back-slapping and laughter among the stalwarts of the gentlemen's chorus, murmurs of approval from many, disappointment from a few. Some extrovert buffoons began to chant 'taran-tara, taran-tara' in anticipation of their approaching duties in the constabulary. Vera and Gladys looked at each other with considerable dismay.

'Quiet, please!' called Desmond, and eventually some semblance of order was restored. Eileen resumed her announcements.

'Auditions for principal parts will be held in three weeks time. Anyone who wants to try for a particular role, please let Doreen know next week, when we begin music rehearsals. You may have your scores and libretti tonight don't forget to sign for them. And Doreen also has the list of audition pieces for those who are interested. Now-Terry has something to say to you all.'

Terry rose elegantly to his feet.

'Lovely to see you all again- and some new faces, too. I'm going to let you all into a secret. We've decided to update 'Pirates' to the 1920s- won't that be fun?'

There was a buzz of interest at this piece of information.

'Something else,' Terry continued, 'this time we're going to ask the ladies' chorus to audition, too- I'm sure you won't mind, dears. Just a short piece from the girls' opening chorus- you know- the 'climbing over rocky mountains' bit- nothing to worry about. But the nineteen-twenties calls for quite a few dance steps, so we'll need to know what you can all do. Thank you so much.'

And Terry sat down, amidst a din of excited conversation, particularly from the ladies, who were somewhat disconcerted to hear that they would have to audition just to be in the chorus. But Desmond cut short the animated chatter by calling everyone to order, and the meeting proceeded smoothly. Fred gave a concise account of the society's current financial position, George emphasised the value of publicity, and how everyone could help with this, and Norma spoke briefly of the style of the 1920s costumes the girls would be wearing. At last all the business was completed and Terry rose once again to speak.

'At the end of next Tuesday's music rehearsal, which concerns everybody,' he said, 'I'm going to ask the girls to stay behind for their auditions. They'll be very brief, so you won't be kept too long. And don't worry- I'm sure you'll all be *wonderful*.'

As Eileen wound up the meeting there was more noisy chatter, and everyone prepared to collect their scores from Sandra before leaving the hall. Beryl Savage and Joan Ormiston, two rather staid altos, looked very glum.

'I wish people would leave Gilbert and Sullivan alone,' said Joan. 'It's all right as it is, performed in the traditional way. Why do people always want to change everything?'

'Goodness knows,' replied Beryl gloomily. 'And- dancing- what-ever does Terry mean? Of course there's dancing- nice dainty steps, pas-bas and waltzing. . . but why audition for that? We've always done that sort of choreography-'

'There's more to it than that,' said Joan darkly. 'Terry's up to something, I'm sure of it. Why don't we go next door for a drink-he's certain to be in the pub, and we may find out a bit more about what he intends to do.'

'All right,' agreed Beryl, 'I don't usually, but this is a matter of some importance. We may not want to be in the show if it's not going to be tasteful, and produced the way it should be.'

'Precisely,' replied Joan. 'Let's find out.'

And they put on their coats, collected their various belongings, and made for the Marleigh Arms, next door to the hall.

Gladys and Vera were still in their seats, slowly putting away their knitting, oblivious of the hubbub around them, and the clatter of Desmond noisily stacking chairs.

'You see, Glad?' said Vera sadly.

'All too plainly,' replied Gladys, zipping up her knitting bag. 'They're after the young ones. You were right.'

'Then let's tell Eileen now,' suggested Vera. 'Let her know we can see that it's time we resigned. She'll understand our position in the light of Terry's new ideas. How could we audition? We'd be a laughing stock.'

Putting on their outdoor clothes, Vera and Gladys waited to intercept Eileen as she left the platform.

'Eileen- can we have a word with you?' called Vera.

Eileen approached the two a little nervously, realising that Terry's audition scheme might have caused offence.

'Certainly, ladies,' she said with a smile, 'what can I do for you?'

'You explain, Vera,' said Gladys.

'Well. . . ' began Vera hesitantly, 'Glad and I have been having a heart-to-heart. When we were discussing what the next show might be, we decided that if it was anything like 'Iolanthe', we'd just have to opt out. After all, we couldn't be fairies any longer, could we?'

 Eileen made to interrupt, but Gladys cut her short.

'No, Eileen- there's no two ways about it. 'Take 'Pirates,'- how can Vera and I be General Stanley's daughters, tell me that?'

'And how could we possibly do an audition, and *dance*?' said Vera.

'We should look ridiculous,' declared Gladys. 'And we're not prepared to.'

Eileen sighed.

'Now, if it had been 'The Yeomen of the Guard',' said Vera, 'we'd have been all right as part of the crowd in the Tower- you need all ages for that. But young girls- 'a bevy of beautiful maidens' I believe they're described as- well, really- me with my varicose veins and Glad with her fallen arches- I ask you!'

'But you've both been with the society for so long,' sighed Eileen, 'Such reliable members and good voices- you *can't* leave us.'

'What do you suggest, then?' said Vera.

'Speak to Terry,' advised Eileen. 'He's got all sorts of ideas, I know. I'm sure there will be something for you. See what he says.'

'All right,' said Gladys. We don't want to leave- of course we don't. But you see our point?'

'Yes,' said Eileen. 'I do. I realise how you're feeling. Now I have to go- but don't forget- have a word with Terry, ladies- I know it'll all work out.'

Eileen went on her way, and Gladys and Vera gathered up their things and followed her.

'Is it worth collecting our scores?' said Gladys despondently.

'Yes,' replied Vera. 'Let's not give up until we have to. You never know. We'll have a word with Terry before the rehearsal next week.'

'All right,' sighed Gladys. 'Now, let's get our scores, and we'll hope for the best.'

CHAPTER 4

The lounge bar of the Marleigh Arms was packed, predominantly with members of the operatic society. Everyone was talking about that evening's events, most particularly Terry's new ideas for the forthcoming production. Some approved, some did not. Terry had miraculously found a table, and was surrounded by people demanding further information, and besieging him with questions.

'Just a minute, folks,' he was protesting, 'one at a time!'

Ian came in with Sue, and the pair fought their way to the bar.

'What a crush,' laughed Ian, 'what'll you have, Sue?'

'Oh, a white wine, please, Ian- dry, if they have it,' she replied, 'that's if you can ever get served.'

Ron Catesby, double scotch in hand, noticed Sue standing alone, and pushed his way through the crowd. Here was a new inexperienced young member to impress- or so he thought.

'Hello, there- new to the society, eh?' he said. 'I'm Ron Catesby- play all the principal tenor roles- I expect you've heard of me. So you're a singer -what voice are you?'

'Oh-er- hello,' replied Sue. 'I'm a soprano-'

'Ha,ha! Thought you'd say that!' laughed Ron. 'All the new females claim to be sopranos- they like singing the tune! Easier, of course. I expect old Jack'll soon have you down on the alto line- they're always short-'

'But I'm quite a high soprano,' protested Sue, looking around desperately for Ian.

'Oh, well- we'll see,' said Ron, 'someone getting you a drink?'

'Yes,' said Sue thankfully, seeing Ian on his way.

'Did you see 'The Gondoliers' over at Cranley Heath last week?' persisted Ron. He did not wait for her to reply. 'Lovely show-plenty of good stuff for the tenor to sing - that was me, of course-'

'Oh- you played Marco? Did you have a good Gianetta?' asked Sue. She was determined to show Ron her considerable knowledge of the Gilbert and Sullivan operas. New she might be. Ignorant she was not.

Ron looked somewhat deflated.

'Oh. . . . so you know your G&S, then?' he said.

'Brought up on it,' answered Sue. 'My mother used to sing all the leads in her local operatic society.'

'I see,' said Ron. 'Have you any ambitions?'

'Not sure yet,' replied Sue. 'I may audition for a principal part, but I wouldn't expect to get one. I'm too new.'

'No chance of playing Mabel, of course. Sandra Ogilvie's been doing all those parts for years. Used to be a damn fine voice-showing signs of wear now, though-' And Ron downed the remains of his scotch in one rather noisy gulp.

'Is she here tonight?' enquired Sue.

'Yes- saw her a few minutes ago- oh, yes- there she is in the far corner, talking to Jack Conway, our musical director.'

'Where?' said Sue, craning her neck to see. 'Oh.. . . so that's Sandra.' Her disappointment was obvious. Mabel should be young, surely?

At that moment Ian turned up with the drinks.

'Sorry to be such an age,' he apologised. 'I got waylaid by Mike Mitchell, and I couldn't get away.' Ian handed Sue her glass of wine and took a long draught of beer. 'Ah, that's better.' He turned to Ron. 'Looking forward to playing Frederic, eh, Ron?'

'*Rather*- know the part backwards. Hardly worth auditioning- just a formality, really.' Ron regarded his empty glass with surprise.

'Can't believe that was a double- they seem a bit stingy with their measures in here lately. Might as well get a refill. How about you?'

'No, we're OK, thanks,' said Ian, and Ron made his way to the bar.

Sue was indignant.

'How can *he* play Frederic? He's supposed to be twenty-one! Ron's at least twice that age- more, if anything.'

'Ssshhh!' cautioned Ian, looking round to see if Sue's remark had been overheard. 'I'm inclined to agree, but you try telling him that! Besides he's a great local favourite- always gets a couple of encores for his big number. The audience went mad when he sang 'Take a pair of sparkling eyes' last week over at Cranley Heath.'

'But what about *you*?' asked Sue. 'You're a tenor- and you're *young-*'

'Not a hope,' replied Ian cheerfully. 'Not with Ron around. There's a small part- Samuel- he's sort of chief pirate. I might get that.'

'I think that's most unfair,' said Sue.

Ian laughed. 'You haven't heard me sing yet!' He took a sip of his beer. 'But I must say Ron's looking his age these days. And he seems to be knocking back the hard stuff lately- there he is with another double scotch.'

'Does he always drink like that?' asked Sue.

'Used not to. I've heard he's got a bit of trouble at home. Mike Mitchell heard his wife had walked out on him- and they've been married twenty years or more.'

'How sad,' said Sue. 'Now, tell me- which is Mike?'

He's over there, talking to Sandra,' replied Ian. 'Marvellous co-median- good timing. You know all those patter songs in G&S? Well, he's really great at all that.'

'And who's that attractive woman with auburn hair- the one by the door, with -Jack Conway-is it? She looks nice.'

'Where? Oh- that's Sheila Allen. Yes, she's OK. Often plays the principal contralto roles- I expect she'll be cast as Ruth.'

Sue gave a sigh. 'Well, if the same people always play the leads, what point is there in holding auditions?'

Ian smiled. 'Oh, looks good, I suppose. They always have a couple of outsiders on the judging panel, but it never seems to make any difference. Come over and meet Sheila. You might as well start getting to know everyone.'

Ian led Sue over to Sheila, a woman in her forties, with striking auburn hair and a pleasant, expressive face.

'Glad you've joined us, Sue,' said Sheila with a friendly smile. 'We can do with some new blood in the society- some of us are getting a bit long in the tooth!'

'Well, at least you're the right age for the parts you play,' said Ian, 'which is more than can be said for some of the others.'

'Ssshh, Ian!' laughed Sheila. Still, I suppose you're right. But it's certainly time *you* had a chance to play a decent part.'

'How can I, with the great Catesby around?' said Ian. 'But I always enjoy the show, whatever I do. God, there goes Ron for another refill- he'll be on his back.'

Sue looked at her watch. 'I think I should be going,' she said, 'I hadn't realised it was so late.'

As she spoke, Mike Mitchell joined the group. Sue regarded him with interest, picturing him in the comedy roles which are always such a feature of the Gilbert and Sullivan operas. He was the right build, and she could imagine him being quite nimble on his feet. Moreover, he had a definite twinkle in his eye which indicated the presence of a good sense of humour.

'Hello, who's going to introduce me to this gorgeous new addition to the society?' he asked, giving Sue a dazzling smile.

'Hands off, Mike!' warned Ian. 'This is Sue Hebden- and I've warned her all about *you*.'

'I see,' said Mike, striking an attitude of mock despair, 'no chance for me now. Never mind. Welcome to Marleigh Operatic Society anyway, Sue. How about a drink?'

'I was just about to go,' replied Sue, 'so, no thank you- another time.' 'Me, too,' said Ian. 'I've got to get up at crack of dawn.'

Sue had noticed a strange change in the atmosphere when Mike appeared on the scene. There was a definite coolness between him and Sheila, who had refused his offer of a drink abruptly- almost rudely- and Sue wondered if it was just that they did not get on with each other, or perhaps had fallen out over some society matter. She would ask Ian later. At that point Ron Catesby barged his way across to them.

'Hi, Sheila! Looking forward to playing Ruth?'

'Don't jump the gun, Ron,' advised Sheila, 'the auditions aren't for three weeks.'

'Oh, it's a foregone conclusion,' said Ron. 'How about *you*, Mike?'

'Might have a go at the Major General,' replied Mike. 'That's song's a bit hair-raising, though. Of all the patter stuff Gilbert wrote, I think that's the worst- even the 'Nightmare Song' from 'Iolanthe's' not so bad, somehow.

Anyway, we'll see.' Ron laughed. 'You'll have to keep off the booze before the show!'

'Oh, I always do,' said Mike. Never touch a drop till afterwards- then I let my hair down.'

Ron slapped him heartily on the back, causing Mike to spill some of his beer, before walking rather unsteadily away to inflict his company on some other unfortunate people. Mike was not amused.

'I wish Ron would layoff the drink,' he grumbled, mopping up the spilt beer from the front of his immaculate sweat shirt.

'Has he got to drive home?' asked Sue.

'I think so,' replied Mike. 'He's in no fit state for that- what is he thinking of? God help him if he's picked up- he's a menace to himself, and to other drivers.'

'He never used to have more than a couple of halves,' said Sheila. 'What's got into him?'

'Didn't you tell me his wife has left him, Mike?' said Ian. 'Poor old Ron.'

Mike nodded. Sheila looked shocked, but said nothing.

'Well, we're off- come on, Sue- I'll walk you to your car,' and with goodnights all round, Ian and Sue went on their way.

'Can I give you a lift home, Sheila?' asked Mike, 'or do you have your car here?'

'No, I haven't, but I'd rather walk, thank you,' answered Sheila, and without another word she turned on her heel and left him. Mike stood gazing after her, a strange and rather lost expression on his face.

In another corner of the bar, Terry, at his table, had been holding court all evening. Prominent among his audience were Angie Greenwood and Sharon Ackroyd, two of the younger members of the society, and Beryl Savage and Joan Ormiston, from the older contingent.

'Tell us more about the auditions, Terry,' begged Angie. 'Do you want *young* girls?'

'And must they be slim?' demanded Sharon, 'Joan says they have to be very sexy-' 'Really, Sharon-' began Joan, crossly, 'I said nothing of the kind-' but Terry interrupted her.

'Goodness, girls- one at a time! Of course, they must *look* young- and being slim *does* help-'

'What shall we have to do at the audition?' Beryl's tone was suspicious.

'Oh, just a few dance steps- ' began Terry.

'*Dance* steps?' Joan's tone was accusing. 'What *sort* of dance steps?'

'There's not usually much dancing in the Gilbert and Sullivan operas.' Beryl was emphatic on this point.

'No, Beryl, not usually,' replied Terry, 'but this time there may be. Remember, we're setting Pirates in the nineteen-twenties- that may entail a bit of the Charleston- I'm sure you'll soon master it-'

'I'm not sure I like the sound of that, do you, Joan?' sniffed Beryl.

'I don't. I can't think why people can't leave things alone,' she replied.

'You're not going to change *everything*, are you, Terry?' persisted Beryl. 'The traditional business is so good-'

Terry shrugged. 'But, ladies- we have to move with the times-'

'Oh, yes!' exclaimed Sharon gleefully, 'Terry's going to set the girls' opening chorus in a disco-'

'With strobe lighting-' added Angie.

Joan nearly had an apoplectic fit at this monstrous idea.

'I should certainly leave the society if anything of that sort went on,' she said, 'wouldn't you, Beryl?'

Beryl agreed. 'I'd go over to Edgley Operatic,' she said primly. 'They're very traditional. Their chorus is always so well drilled- it's lovely to see.'

'But isn't it a bit dull,' said Angie, 'always doing the same old productions?'

'I agree,' said Sharon. 'The Gilbert and Sullivan operas need a new look, I think.'

'They were good enough for W.S. Gilbert, who first produced them,' said Beryl icily.

'That was over a hundred years ago!' giggled Sharon.

'And don't forget, Beryl, he was way ahead of his time- his productions were topical, and right up to date,' said Terry. 'He'd probably be horrified to think we were still doing his operas the same old way.'

'Well, I don't think you can beat a lovely neat semi-circle of chorus, all doing exactly the same thing on the same beat of the bar,' said Joan.

Terry smiled. 'Oh, I think that sort of thing's gone out now.'

Beryl looked hostile. 'You do?' she said grimly.

Terry nodded. 'Movement and dance and innovation are here to stay, particularly with regard to Gilbert and Sullivan. The operettas we've been doing in recent years have no set production, so we've been able to give each one a fresh new look. But now that we've come back to G&S, which has so much tradition, we must see what we can do to enliven and enrich it.'

'I see,' said Joan, though it was pretty obvious that she didn't. 'Are you ready, Beryl?' 'Yes. Well, we'll see you all next week.' said Beryl in a tone that implied that it might be for the last time. And the two swept out with considerable dignity.

Sharon and Angie burst into loud giggles. Terry was quick to admonish them.

'Hush, girls, we mustn't alienate the traditional school- merely try to win them over. Those are two good altos, my dears- we must hang on to them at all costs. They're not two a penny like all you sopranos!'

'Well, really, Terry-' began Angie.

'Cheek!' protested Sharon. 'Oh, watch it, Angie- here's Ron coming this way.'

With a rather lurching gait Ron approached the two girls and put an arm round each.

'My two favourite young ladies!' he murmured in slurred tones, then burst into Frederic's first song from Pirates, giving it quite another meaning from the intended one.

'Oh, is there not one maiden breast-' he sang loudly and coarsely, moving his hands suggestively in the appropriate direction.

The girls edged away, laughing with embarrassment.

'Stop that, Ron,' protested Angie, 'not here!'

'Why not?' said Ron, 'you'll be the two sexiest daughters of General Stanley ever to grace the stage! Mind you,' he reflected, 'that new fair-haired piece isn't too bad-'

'Sue Hebden?' said Terry. Yes- she'll be quite an asset. And we hope to have one or two more young ones joining us in the next couple of weeks. We've done a real recruitment drive.'

'Good-oh,' said Ron, licking his lips. 'I look forward to that. Glad you chose 'Pirates'- plenty of scope for my talents- in all directions,' he added, winking lasciviously at the girls. 'Suppose I'd better hit the road, 'bye, all- see you next week.' And he made his way unsteadily to the door.

'He may well 'hit the road' literally,' said Angie in disgust, 'and another car, too, if he's going to drive in that state.'

He's certainly had more than a drop too much,' agreed Terry anxiously, 'hope he'll be OK.'

'Come on, Angie,' said Sharon, 'or they'll throw us out. 'Night, Terry- we'd better give our dancing shoes an airing before we meet again. Is it ballet or tap?'

'Both,' laughed Terry, 'with a spot of acrobatic thrown in! I must go, too.'

Everyone seemed to be leaving at once, and there was a lot of noise and laughter as the crowd spilled out into the car park

'Brrrr, it's cold,' said Angie, as she and Sharon made their way to Angie's car. Suddenly there was a loud revving of an engine, and a car accelerated wildly towards the two girls. Terry, just behind them, shouted in panic,

'Watch it, Sharon, for God's sake,' and grabbing hold of her, pulled her to one side just in time, nearly throwing her to the ground.

Sharon screamed in alarm, clutching Terry fearfully. 'Oh, God- that was close! Silly bastard- what the hell did he think he was doing?'

Terry tried to soothe her. '1 don't think he had a clue what he was doing,' he said bitterly.

'He nearly ran me down,' Sharon sobbed.

'Are you all right?' asked Angie anxiously, bending down to retrieve Angie's score and bag from the ground where they had fallen.

'Yes- thanks to Terry,' said Sharon. 'He pulled me clear just in time- did you get the idiot's number?' Terry was white with anger.

'No need,' he said quietly. I *know* who it was. It was Ron Catesby.'

CHAPTER 5

The first music rehearsal of Marleigh's next production, 'The Pirates of Penzance', had just ended, and the male members of the cast were preparing to leave the hall, most bound for the pub next door. The ladies, however, stood around in apprehensive groups, awaiting their imminent auditions. Everyone had turned up for the rehearsal that evening for the sing-through of the show, some of the prospective principals filling in the solo parts. Ron had loudly sung all Frederic's music, but it was noticed that Sandra had not attempted any of Mabel's. When the rehearsal pianist, Janet Evans, had played her big number 'Poor Wand'ring One', Sandra had remained silent.

One or two people had looked expectantly at her, among them Jack Conway, who was conducting. Sandra, however, appeared not to notice, and continued to gaze at her score, seemingly deep in concentration. As the men filed out, there were some shouts of encouragement to the nervous audition candidates, and also a few facetious pieces of advice. Vera and Gladys waited to speak to Terry. They both looked serious, and very worried. Angie and Sharon, and one or two of the younger girls were trying out a few impromptu dance steps with a lot of giggling, until, after a particularly high kick, Sharon collapsed on the floor in helpless laughter. Joan and Beryl, looking grim, watched with disapproval, but Sue and Sheila, also waiting to try out their footwork for Terry, applauded enthusiastically.

'Has Sandra gone?' asked Sheila, looking round.

'I think so. I saw her leave with Fred just now,' said Sue. 'Perhaps she doesn't need to do the dancing audition.'

'Well, that's a bit much,' complained Sheila. 'All the girls should be here. Nobody's a principal yet- ,we may all end up in the chorus!'

Terry, having finished a consultation with Jack and Doreen, bade them goodnight, and approached the girls. Vera and Gladys blocked his way.

'Hello, ladies, what can I do for you?' he asked, suspecting he already knew.

'I think you *know*,' said Gladys. 'You surely don't expect Vera and me to do a dance audition, do you?'

'Because we *can't*, and what's more, we won't,' declared Vera.

Terry looked at the two women standing somewhat belligerently before him, and his heart gave a twinge. They had made a tremendous effort. Both wore pleated skirts, blouses and cardigans. Vera had forced her feet into court shoes and had obviously had her hair done; Gladys had drawn the line at wearing heels, but had rather inexpertly applied an auburn rinse to her grey hair, which gave a slightly piebald effect. Both, unusually, wore lipstick, and Vera had experimented with some turquoise blue eye shadow.

'I never intended that you *should* audition,' said Terry, 'and I was just about to say so. There are several of you more mature ladies in the society, and we value your contribution to the shows. You are two useful altos, who always turn up, know your parts, and are thoroughly reliable. But, in the case of 'Pirates', you obviously can't be General Stanley's daughters, now, can you?' Gladys and Vera shook their heads despondently.

'However,' continued Terry, 'I have ideas for introducing other characters-'

'How *can* you?' demanded Gladys suspiciously, 'the ladies' chorus is made up of young girls-'

'Yes,' agreed Terry, 'but as they enter the cove, is there any reason why they shouldn't be followed by a couple of servants carrying picnic things? After all, it's hardly likely that young girls in the 20s- the daughters of Major General Stanley, at that- would be allowed to roam around un-chaperoned, is it? There would be a governess, too, probably, and maybe a couple of manservants- they could come on behind the Major General-' Terry's imagination was fired, and Vera and Gladys were beginning to see the possibilities in store.

'But would we *sing*?' asked Vera anxiously.

'*Sing*?' I should think you would!' said Terry. 'And there would be extra bits of business for you- I wouldn't be surprised if we could get you credited in the programme, too. Oh, you'll see- there'll be lots for you to do.'

The two women looked at each other. Relief was evident in their faces.

'All right, Terry,' said Gladys. 'We'll leave it to you.'

'OK, ladies- now go and learn your music- not that you need to, I'm sure-'

'No,' replied Vera, 'we did it in 1978!'

'There you are, then,' laughed Terry, 'See what I mean!'

The two women joined in his laughter, and arm in arm went off to get their coats.

'Well. that's one hurdle over,' thought Terry thankfully, 'now for the other girls.'

As it turned out, he need not have worried. The audition candidates, taken one by one in an adjoining room, proved to be very amenable to his simple dance steps. Even Joan and Beryl caught on quickly, actually seeming to enjoy the experience, although they would never have admitted it. With the exception of a couple of older ladies, all the girls made the grade. Terry took the two of them aside and told them what he had in mind for them, sketching in his ideas as he had done for Gladys and Vera.

"Well done, girls,' he said as he finally dismissed them. 'Don't forget- principal auditions are in two weeks' time- there are three small parts to be cast, as well as the leading ones, so be sure and to learn the music and dialogue in plenty of time.'

'Yes, Terry- goodnight, Terry,' was the response as everyone left the hall.

'And now for the principal auditions,' he mused, as the door closed behind the last candidate. 'I only hope they're as painless as this evening's.'

Audition day dawned at last. Sue Hebden sat at her dressing table gazing into the mirror, lost in thought. She looked up as her mother came in.

'D'you really think I ought to audition for Mabel?' she asked anxiously. 'I'm such a new member of the society- perhaps it'd be better if I stayed in the chorus for the time being, at least-'

'Nonsense,' replied Julia Hebden. She regarded her daughter with a mixture of feelings, seeing herself twenty or so years ago, so full of enthusiasm and promise. If only things had been different- if only Sue's father, her beloved Alan, had not been killed in that horrific accident on the icy motorway three years ago. . . . How he would have loved to see his daughter tonight, so pretty, her cheeks flushed with anticipation. .. But this would not do- Alan was no longer there to support her. Sue needed all the encouragement she could give her. Julia pulled herself together, and spoke in a matter-of-fact voice.

'You've worked so hard at that song, Sue, and you really do sing it beautifully. It'd be a shame not to let them hear you. You may not get the leading role this time, but never mind. Anyway, there are a couple of small parts you could do if not. See what happens.'

'Couldn't have done it without *you*, Mum,' said Sue gratefully. 'You're always ready to drop anything and sit down at the piano. Yes- I'll do it for you, if not for any other reason. But Sandra always plays the principal soprano role, you know she does. I believe she has the most wonderful voice.'

'That's as maybe,' said her mother. 'But you can't go on playing juvenile parts for ever. One of these days they're going to have to find a successor, so you may as well let them know that *you* can sing, too. And what about- what was his name- Ian- is he going to audition for Frederic?'

Sue laughed. 'Well, he's going to have a go, but there again, there's Ron Catesby! Oh, Mum, you should see him! He's got a good tenor voice, I suppose- if you like that sort of thing- but no finesse. He just sings at the top of his voice, and his acting is so *ham* . . . . . . Apparently he's a great local favourite, and swaggers about on stage a treat- but he's supposed to be twenty-one! Surely no amount of makeup can achieve that!'

The two of them went into fits of laughter at this. It was probably the best thing Sue could have done, for her nerves disappeared and she began to feel relaxed, and to look forward to the audition.

'Do I look OK, Mum?' she asked, putting on her coat and wrapping a scarf round her neck.

'Wonderful,' replied her mother proudly. 'Now, have a good time, and give them all you've got!'

Sue blew her a kiss and hurried out to her car, eager to be on her way.

Things were not so relaxed at Sandra's home. Seated at the piano, she was working on the song she would have to sing that evening, without much success. Over and over again she tried the difficult passages, missing the top notes and failing to produce the agility so essential for the florid passages. 'Poor Wand'ring One', Mabel's big aria, the showpiece the audience is waiting for is one of the high points of the show. It has to be sung with precision as well as charm, and is often encored. Sandra knew all this well- had she not done just that so many years ago? She still possessed a very good voice, and considerable appeal on stage,. but the part of Mabel demanded more than she appeared able to give. She made one more attempt to hit the final top Db, missed it, slammed down the piano lid and burst into tears.

She heard Fred's key turn in the lock; the front door opened and closed.

'Sandra! I'm home-' Fred poked his head round the sitting room door. 'Hello, love- practising for the audition? Hey- what's up?'

Fred saw with great concern that all was not well with his wife. Tears coursed down her face, and she looked at him despairingly.

'It's no use, Fred,' she said.

'Whatever do you mean?' He stared at her. This wasn't the Sandra he knew.

'I never wanted us to do 'Pirates',' she sobbed. 'I expected this might happen. I'm finished- oh, what shall I do, what *shall* I do-'

Fred went and put his arms around her, holding her tightly to him.

'Now, listen, love,' he said soothingly, 'd'you know something? I bet if you go to the audition tonight, those notes you're worried about'll come back like magic. You know how you always rise to the occasion on first nights- everyone else as nervous as hell, and there you are- cool as a cucumber, giving a marvellous performance. I've watched you so many times. . . . .'

'Oh, Fred- I can't go to the audition, I simply can't-'

'Nonsense! I've never heard of anything so silly. You can, and you will.'

Sandra made a faint gesture of protest, but Fred broke in.

'You'll see, love- it'll be just as I say. Now, go and dress yourself up- and put on plenty of makeup- you'll be as right as rain. Who on earth is there for Mabel if not you?'

Sandra was unconvinced, but she was weakening under the force of Fred's persuasion.

'OK.' she said wearily at last. 'Maybe you're right.'

'I know I'm right.' Fred was adamant.

'Your supper's in the oven,' she said, 'I can't eat anything-'

'Don't you worry at all, I'll see to it. What time do you have to leave?'

Fred's voice was cheery and confident.

'Oh- in about half an hour,' replied Sandra, her tone still doubtful.

'I'll make you a nice cup of tea before you go- strong and sweet-that'll put you right. Now, don't worry.'

'All right, Fred.' Sandra gave her husband a watery smile and went to see what she could do to repair the ravages the fit of weeping had done to her face. Fred, reassured that he had done the right thing, bustled off to the kitchen.

There was a hum of excited voices and plenty of nervous laughter at the church hall that evening. Sometimes the distant sound of a piano could be heard, but as the audition room was down a corridor and round the corner, nothing much of what was going on there was audible. In the main hall, which served as a waiting room, some of the hopeful ones were muttering their dialogue in corners, and from the gentlemen's loo came the occasional somewhat strained notes of an aspiring tenor. Sue was chatting to Sheila when Ian arrived, score under his arm, a bit out of breath.

'Hey, you lot have taken all the parking spaces,' he complained jokingly. 'Don't you know you're supposed to leave one for the principal tenor?'

A series of catcalls greeted this statement, and Doreen, bustling in with a list of names, called for less noise.

'Goodness, what a racket!' she said, 'we can hear you in the audition room - less noise, please!'

'Oh, Doreen, stop fussing like a mother hen!' said Mike Mitchell, 'and tell us who's next.'

'Major Generals,' announced Doreen. 'And you can be first, Mike.'

'Me?' said Mike in disbelief. '*First*? Oh well- might as well get it over.'

And he staggered away in Doreen's wake, pretending to be in deep shock.

'Hi, Sharon,' said Ian, joining the group of girls. 'Trying for Mabel?'

'You must be joking,' she said. 'I'm hoping for one of the small parts- Edith, or Kate. So is Angie.'

'You bet,' agreed Angie. 'We couldn't get near Mabel. Besides, that's a foregone conclusion-'

'Not necessarily,' replied Ian. 'There are several new girls this season. We shall have to see what they can do- you never know.' And he winked at Sue.

Sharon noted this, and pulled Angie away from the group.

'Well, really! Is she trying for Mabel? What a nerve- she's only been in the society five minutes-'

Angie gave a derisive laugh. 'Oh, I don't suppose she's got much of a voice- Sandra'll be here soon. She'll walk away with it.'

'But she must have quite an opinion of herself-' Sharon was indignant.

Angie agreed. 'She'll learn. Wait till she hears Sandra. That'll show her.'

Ian crept up behind the girls and made them jump.

'What are you whispering about, you two? Let me in on the scandal!'

'Go away, Ian- it's girls' talk!' And Sharon pushed Ian away.

At that moment Doreen re-appeared on the scene with her list, Mike following behind in an assumed state of collapse.

'Phew!' he said, fanning himself with his libretto, 'what a traumatic experience! Don't go in there, anyone, if you value your lives!'

'Thanks very much,' said Ian. 'Now we feel really confident.'

'Any more Major Generals here?' enquired Doreen, consulting her list. 'Oh, yes- Cyril- that's right, come along- bring your score if you need it.'

And away went Cyril Higgins in hopeful mood, though it would have been impossible to imagine a less military figure.

Sue had strolled over to the notice board to see the order of auditions, which nobody seemed to have consulted. She was joined by Sharon and Angie.

'Have you done much singing before?' asked Sharon casually.

'Not an awful lot,' replied Sue. 'I've been having lessons for a couple of years-'

'Mabel's a terribly difficult part, you know,' remarked Angie pointedly.

'Yes. I know-' began Sue.

'Not the sort of role for a beginner,' said Angie.

Sue could see the way the conversation was angled, and was not afraid to answer back.

'Well, we all have to start some time, don't we?' she answered sweetly. 'No good waiting till we're past it.'

Sharon looked at Angie. 'Sandra here yet?' she asked casually.

'Not yet. Should be, any time now.' said Angie.

'She's wonderful,' Sharon informed Sue. Such a voice. And a marvellous actress, too.'

'I'm sure she is,' was Sue's unruffled reply. '1 shall look forward to hearing her.'

'You will,' Angie said. 'As Mabe1. 'Come on, Sharon.' And the two girls strolled off.

Sue took a deep breath. She would not lose her temper, she would not get upset, she would keep her cool. More important, she would go into the audition room and sing as she had never sung before. She was about to go and find Ian when Doreen appeared once more, calling for the candidates for the role of Frederic.

'Frederics now, please- Arthur Dobbs, you're first on the list-'

A short, stocky chap of indeterminate age came forward. 'Right-oh, love,' he said cheerfully in a strong Leeds accent, 'lets get going.'

And away they went, Doreen calling over her shoulder, 'Stand by, Ian- you're next.'

'Oh God,' cried Ian, 'I wish I'd never entered for this- it's all a big mistake-'

Sue burst out laughing. 'You're supposed to be doing this for fun, remember? I wonder how Sheila got on- she went in earlier- ah, here she is. How do you think you did, Sheila- is it in the bag?'

'Well, we'll know soon enough,' was the reply. 'It was OK, I think.'

'You mean, they'll let us know tonight?' Sue asked in surprise.

'Oh yes, they usually do. They don't like to keep us in suspense too long,' replied Sheila.

'What if you don't get the part?' asked Ian.

'Well, I'll just have to be in the chorus- if I'm young and pretty enough,' she laughed.

'Here comes Doreen now,' said Sue. 'Your turn, Ian- good luck!'

'Yes, that's right,' said Doreen. 'You're after Ian, Hamish.'

This last remark was addressed to a gaunt tenor with a marked Scottish accent; it was hard to imagine him as a dashing young lover.

'Ian's got a damn good voice- it's time he had a chance to do a principal role soon,' said Mike, who had joined the group. 'Still, with Ron around. . . '

'Talk of the devil,' said Sheila, as the great Ron Catesby himself sailed into the room.

'Good evening, fellow thespians- am I on cue?' And Ron turned his famous smile upon the assembled company.

'Hello, Ron. After Hamish, I think,' said Sheila. 'Ian's in there now.'

'Good old Ian. He'll make a fine Samuel-' Ron burst into song. 'Pour, oh pour the pirate sherry- fill, oh fill the pirate glass-' He warbled the words of the opening chorus resonantly and dramatically, with appropriate gestures. 'Could do with a drop of that just now, to oil the vocal chords-' and Ron swept away to impress another group of candidates.

'1 should think he's had more than a drop already,' whispered Sue to Sheila.

Doreen called, 'Hamish McRae- will you come now, please?'

'Och, aye, Doreen- I'll awa' and show them how it should be sung!' said Hamish, following her out of the hall.

'Fancy singing a love duet with him!' sniggered Sharon.

'Those teeth would get in the way a bit when it came to the kiss,' said Angie.

'Now, now, girls,' said Ian, who had just returned to the hall, 'Hamish has a fine tenor voice!'

'That's not all you need!' giggled Sharon.

'He might be good in Brigadoon,' suggested Sue. 'Oh. Ian-how did you get on?'

'Not too bad, thanks, Sue- didn't disgrace myself, anyway. Feel like a drink, Mike? We could go next door for one- they'll be at least another half hour or so with these auditions.'

'Good idea,' replied Mike. 'Are you coming, Sheila?'

'No thanks, Mike. I prefer to stay here.' She turned away from him.

'Oh. . . ' Mike was disconcerted. 'Well, you come and join us, Sue, when you're done?'

'I will. I shall certainly need it!' said Sue.

Doreen appeared at the door.

'Ah, Doreen, my beloved- has the great call come?'

'It has,' she replied, totally unmoved by Ron's histrionics.

'Right. Take a pair of sparkling eyes-' warbled Ron in full voice. 'Oh, sorry- wrong opera!' And he made a dramatic exit as everyone laughed at his antics.

'I wonder how many he's had?' said Sharon.

'God knows,' replied Angie in exasperation. 'I hope he's a bit more careful driving. I met him in the High Street the other day and tore him off a strip for nearly knocking you down that night.'

'Good. What did he say?' asked Sharon.

'Oh- that his steering needed a bit of attention.'

'You can say that again,' said Sharon with feeling.

The auditions went on apace, and before long it was Sue's turn. She went off to the audition room coolly, and seemed to be kept longer than most.

Sharon and Angie strained their ears to try and hear her, but there was too much noise in the hall. Eventually she re-appeared, seeming quite self-possessed. The two girls stared at her curiously, but her face gave nothing away.

'All right, Sue?' asked Sheila, but Sue merely smiled and nodded.

Doreen was getting agitated. 'Anyone seen Sandra?' she asked. As she spoke, the door to the street burst open, and Sandra appeared, her face tense, oblivious to the smiles and greetings from her friends.

'Right on cue!' said Doreen, with relief. 'You're next, Sandra.' And without a word Sandra followed her out of the hall.

'Funny!' said Angie. 'I've never seen Sandra look like that.'

'Nor I. She's always got a smile for everyone- especially at audition time- likes to give people encouragement-' Sharon was puzzled.

'Oh, maybe she had some trouble with her car, and was running late- she'll no doubt have a chat afterwards,' said Angie.

But in a few minutes the door burst open and Sandra ran in, dishevelled and appearing distressed. She gazed wildly round the hall, apparently seeing no-one, then as Sheila made a movement towards her, rushed out of the main door into the street. Everyone stood rooted to the spot, unable to comprehend the situation. What was the matter with Sandra, their leading lady?

CHAPTER 6

As the door slammed shut behind Sandra there was a stunned silence in the hall. After a few moments Mike Mitchell gave a low whistle.

'Wow!' exclaimed Sharon with, feeling.

'What's got into *her*?' said Ian.

Sheila, who had hurried after Sandra, returned, looking anxious.

'I tried to catch her before she left, but I was too late. She jumped into her car and drove off at high speed- oh, I do hope she'll be all right. I've never seen her so upset- what on earth could have happened?'

A general buzz of speculative conversation followed Sheila's statement, and it was obvious that everyone was puzzled at Sandra's strange behaviour.

'What can be going on?' Sue asked Ian. 'You know all these people much better than I do. Does Sandra often indulge in such histrionics?'

'Far from it,' replied Ian. 'I'm as surprised as you are. She's usually relaxed and friendly- never a drama queen. Can't think what's got into her.'

The door into the corridor opened and Eileen came into the hall. She looked worried and ill at ease. All chatter ceased at her appearance, and everyone waited to hear what she had to say.

'We'd like to thank you all very much for coming tonight, and for your impressive auditions. We are fortunate to have so much talent to choose from, but it means that we are having an almost impossible task making our final decisions.' Eileen smiled nervously at everyone. 'As you know, the audition panel usually let you know the results at once, but this year we really do need extra time. So I ask your indulgence and your understanding when I tell you that the cast list will not be available tonight.' A groan of disappointment greeted Eileen's words, but she gamely went on.

'Anyone who really can't wait until next Tuesday's rehearsal for the results may phone me on Saturday evening, when I shall be able to put you out of your suspense. Thank you all so much.' And Eileen disappeared whence she had come.

'How on earth shall I be able to wait?' laughed Ron, who had just rolled in from the Marleigh Arms, and who knew with absolute confidence that the leading tenor role was his- as always.

Disappointed murmurs greeted Eileen's words, and people began to put on coats, collect scores, and prepare to leave. There was none of the excitement normally associated with audition night, and the whole event seemed to end with an air of anti-climax. A general move towards the Marleigh Arms was soon in evidence, where the topic of discussion would no doubt be the unusual happenings that had just taken place.

'What a strange evening,' remarked Ian, as he and Sue made their way to the bar. 'We'd normally know who the stars of our next show are going to be by now. And Eileen looked decidedly embarrassed, I thought. I wonder what's really going on- white wine, Sue?'

'Yes- dry, please. Do you think it could be something to do with Sandra?' wondered Sue. 'That was rather a dramatic exit she made- wouldn't she normally wait to hear the cast list read out? I mean, not for her own sake- that's a foregone conclusion- but to hear who the others are?'

'Yes, she would,' said Ian, handing Sue her glass. 'I'd like to be a fly on the wall in that audition room right now.'

The panel of adjudicators sat round the table looking weary and dispirited.

Terry Althorpe, deep in thought, stared unseeingly at his cast list, and Jack Conway drummed his fingers incessantly on his score. Eileen, a worried expression on her face. gazed at the opposite wall, deep in thought. The two members from outside the society examined their notes studiously, pencilling in additional comments here and there.

Doreen relieved the intensity of the atmosphere by arriving noisily on the scene with a tray of coffee, which was thankfully received. By the time milk, sugar and custard creams had been passed round, everyone had relaxed slightly.

'Well- what a turn-up for the book,' said Terry, helping himself to a second biscuit. 'And to quote from 'The Mikado'- 'Here's a pretty how-de-do'!'

'Yes- no-one expected a problem like this,' said Jack. stirring his coffee for the third time.

'Let's start with the characters we can cast without any problems,' ventured Eileen, determined to put off for as long as possible the question that was in everyone's mind.

'Good idea,' agreed Jack. 'There were some excellent candidates, but I don't think it will be too difficult to select the successful ones. Take Major General Stanley, for instance- in my opinion, no-one comes anywhere near Mike Mitchell-'

There was unanimous enthusiasm for this piece of casting.

'Yes, he's got exactly the right sort of voice for those roles,' observed Jonathan Wilkes. 'A good light baritone with clear diction, which is not easy where that patter song is concerned. He made a good job of it - 'fluffed' a couple of odd words- but that was probably due to nerves.'

'He's a good actor,' said Hilary. 'With a nice sense of timing, and I liked his characterisation very much.'

'I couldn't agree more,' said Eileen. 'Terry?'

'Oh, it's definitely Mike for me,' enthused Terry. 'Always knows his work, too. There's nobody else, as far as I'm concerned. Let's pencil him in.'

'Next- the Pirate King,' said Eileen. 'Any ideas?'

'Oh, yes,' said Jonathan Wilkes, consulting his list. 'Chris Hatton, surely. What a fine bass voice that is- and he knows what he's doing with it.'

'He really did read extremely well,' added Hilary. 'And he's a very strong character.'

'Tall, too,' said Terry appreciatively. 'And a good presence. Yes, he's definitely my choice.'

'Oh, yes, undoubtedly.' Jack was enthusiastic. 'Chris is a splendid all-round artist.'

'I agree,' said Eileen. 'Now, there's Samuel, his lieutenant. I suppose Ian Richardson could play that. We usually try to give him something to do- must hang on to these good-looking young men.'

'That's fine by me,' said Terry. 'I think Ian's got a lot more talent than he's had a chance to display yet. We must keep him interested- I'm sure he's going to be very valuable to us in the future. Yes, he must certainly have that role- that's if you others are in agreement?' He looked enquiringly at Hilary and Jonathan.

There was general assent, and Ian's name was added to the list.

'Now we come to the Sergeant of the Police,' announced Eileen. 'We've several possibilities, I believe. Jack?'

'Ye-es,' pondered Jack. 'There's no doubt that Keith Lloyd has the best voice, don't you think, Jonathan?'

Without a doubt,' was the answer.

'It's a lovely sound,' added Eileen.

'But do we *need* a lovely sound for the Sergeant?' asked Terry. 'Keith's got absolutely no sense of comedy- sang that song absolutely straight, and I don't believe he could do it any other way. It was like an aria from 'The Messiah.'

Hilary nodded. 'I think he'd have a problem with the characterisation.'

'Then who do you suggest, Terry?' asked Eileen.

'It may surprise you,' said Terry, 'but I do believe that Reg Jennings would be a marvellous Sergeant. He's so droll- you can see from his facial expressions that he knows what it's all about. What do you others think?'

Jonathan ran his eye down his notes. 'His voice is quite good,' he said. 'More than adequate for the demands of the role. I see what you mean, Terry- yes- I believe he'd do very well.'

'Oh, I liked him,' said Hilary. 'He made me laugh- and isn't that what you want?'

'It's an interesting idea,' said Eileen. 'And it's time he had a chance of a substantial part- he's been a good society member for years.'

'I'm happy with that,' agreed Jack. 'But isn't he a bit short and fat?'

'But don't you see, we can use those physical attributes to advantage in that particular role?' enthused Terry. 'He'll be a really comical character, and when he confronts the Pirate King at the end, it'll be a scream!'

Everyone joined in the laughter at the picture Terry conjured up, and saw the logic of his choice.

'Now, Frederic,' said Eileen. 'Does Ron have any contestants?'

There was an audible sniff from Doreen at this.

'Oh, no- I don't think so,' said Jack. 'The audience will expect to see Ron- he has such a fan club around here.'

'What about the age business?' enquired Hilary, who had done her homework on the script. 'It's constantly mentioned throughout the show that he's twenty-one. D'you really think he'll be able to get away with that?'

'Oh, Ron can get away with anything,' said Terry. 'He's outrageous, of course, but the audience adore him.'

'I admit it's a big tenor voice,' said Jonathan, 'but a bit out of hand at times, and beginning to show signs of wear. And he makes such a meal of the high notes-'

'Oh, I'll cope with that,' said Jack. 'We really must have Ron- he's a great local character.'

So, in spite of a few reservations, Ron's name was put down for Frederic.

'Now, what about Ruth?' asked Eileen. 'We had- let me see- four candidates for that role. Personally, I thought Sheila Armstrong was outstanding.'

'Ruth's quite a high mezzo part,' observed Jonathan thoughtfully. 'Two of the others were too plummy, and the third was really a soprano. Yes- Sheila's a natural mezzo, and the role suits her.'

'It does,' said Hilary. 'And she has a good idea of the character.'

'I'd be very happy with Sheila,' said Jack.

Terry nodded. 'So would I. She's my choice, without a doubt. Now, what about those three small parts- Edith, Kate and Isabel? We need three young attractive 'flappers', full of personality and animation,'

'Sharon and Angie spring immediately to mind,' smiled Jack. 'I think Sharon could cope very well with Edith, but Angie's not such a good singer- how about giving her the speaking part of Isabel? She'd be good at that- she read the dialogue beautifully, I thought.' Everyone was of the same opinion.

Jonathan scanned his notes, then said, 'I've got a tick against Lisa Preston. I thought she sang Kate's solo really well. That's a promising young voice.'

Terry seconded that. 'And she's pretty, too. What's more, she does a mean Charleston!' Lisa was decided upon without further debate. So far, the casting of The Pirates of Penzance had been simple and straightforward. Things were about to change.

Eileen took a deep breath. 'About Mabel-' she began.

Jonathan cleared his throat. He knew he was on dangerous ground, and must tread carefully. He cleared his throat.

'There were only two candidates for this vital role,' he said. 'One could sing it, and one could not.'

Eileen made an effort to interrupt, but Jonathan continued, determined to express his views strongly. He was resolved not to give way on this important piece of casting as he had been obliged to over the choice of Ron, who could at least cope with the vocal demands of his role.

'The one who could not was Sandra. It's as simple as that.'

'Oh, but it isn't,' broke in Eileen desperately. 'Sandra's our leading lady- she always plays the principal role-'

Doreen had no right to express any opinion regarding the auditions, being there purely in her secretarial capacity, but could not resist a sardonic laugh at Eileen's intervention.

'As musical director,' said Jack, who could see that a firm hand was needed here, 'I'm bound to agree with Jonathan that Sandra just can't sing the role. Couldn't get near those top notes- missed 'em by a mile.-'

'But, Jack-' said Eileen wildly, 'Perhaps she has a cold- a sore throat-'

'Nonsense!' replied Jack. 'It's simply beyond her. We gave her a couple of shots at it. Sopranos do tend to lose their top notes as they get older.'

Eileen would not give up. 'But she's such a good actress-' she looked to other members of the panel for support, but no-one would meet her eyes.

'You can't cover up poor singing with histrionics, Eileen,' said Jack gently, 'Certainly not where Mabel's concerned.'

'Jack's right, of course,' sighed Terry. 'And it's not as if we can't cast the role. There's young Sue Hebden- she sang that song like an angel.'

'Pretty, too. And young,' Doreen could not resist adding.

'But what can we do about Sandra?' It'll destroy her,' said Eileen. 'The operatic society's her life. She spends six months of the year practising and rehearsing, and the other six looking back at the last show and looking forward to the next.'

'I know, that's what's so awful,' sighed Terry. 'Hilary- we haven't heard from you yet- what's your opinion?'

Hilary looked serious. 'Of course, Sandra's a very good actress. We all know that- we've seen her do so many excellent things in the past. But, singing apart- I find her too-er- mature - for Mabel.

Dramatically and physically I would unhesitatingly choose Sue Hebden.'

'I agree totally,' said Jonathan. 'Good heavens, what more do you want? Sue sang delightfully. She is young and pretty. The society is fortunate to have her.'

'Hear, hear,' said Jack. 'I'm afraid we must leave sentiment out of it and choose the best talent we have available. Sue is outstanding, and deserves the part.'

Eileen made a last-ditch effort. 'But she's only just joined-'

Doreen could not restrain herself. 'What does that matter? She's paid her subscription, attended rehearsals, and is just as eligible as anyone else.'

'Doreen's right, I'm afraid, Eileen,' said Terry. 'We appreciate your feelings, sympathise with them, even- but we must have the best voice for the part.'

Jonathan felt it was time to take a firm stand. 'Look,' he said, 'I'm going to be really brutal, in the interests of the society and the show. You have two choices: a middle-aged soprano who simply is way past her best, or a very attractive young singer, well-equipped vocally, and showing enormous promise. Sandra would have to give up some time, and it's pretty obvious that time is now.'

There was an uncomfortable silence after Jonathan's outspoken remarks, though all the members of the panel knew in their hearts that he had merely spoken the truth.

In the face of such opposition, Eileen capitulated.

'Oh dear, I suppose you're right. But who's going to break the news to Sandra?'

'I don't suppose anyone needs to,' observed Jack. 'She's no fool- she'll know, after tonight's events.'

'We have our list of principals, then,' announced Doreen in business-like manner. 'I'll get it typed up.'

'Wait a minute-' said Terry, 'You don't think Sandra would settle for Edith?'

'A small part?' exclaimed Eileen, horrified. 'Oh no, that would be cruel-'

'It would,' said Jack. 'But everyone has to give up some time. Sandra's had a very good innings.'

'I think the cast list sounds very promising,' said Hilary. 'I look forward to seeing the show.'

'Good. Shall we call it a day, then?' said Jack, stifling a yawn, and leaning back in his chair with a satisfied expression.

'I suppose we must. But a very sad one,' said Eileen unhappily. 'I'll have to call and let Sandra know tomorrow- it'll have to be in the afternoon- I've a hair appointment in the morning. So I shall see you then, Terry, and perhaps you can help me with what to say to her.'

'Of course, love,' said Terry, patting Eileen's shoulder comfortingly. 'We'll see what we can come up with.'

'Well, thank you all for your valuable advice and co-operation tonight,' said Jack. 'It's been an unusually difficult session, but I'm sure we've got things sorted out now.' There was agreement from everyone but Eileen, who still looked very unhappy. She did not relish her encounter with Sandra the following day.

CHAPTER 7

Fred woke up with a start, and shivered. The television was mumbling on, but the sitting room was cold, and he wondered why the central heating was off. Rubbing his eyes, he peered at the clock- it *couldn't* be- twenty past *three*! Where was Sandra? She would never have come in and gone up to bed without waking him- he called her name, knowing there would be no reply. All was silent. Then what had happened? Fred's heart began to race, his mind conjuring up all sorts of things. There must have been an accident- was Sandra in hospital? No, that was silly- he would have been contacted by now. What should he do? He must ring Terry. Blindly he searched for the phone number, and tapped it in, his fingers all thumbs. It seemed an eternity before Terry's sleepy voice answered.

'Yes? Hello- what on earth?'

'Terry, oh Terry- it's me- Fred-'

'Who? What? oh- Fred? Good God, do you know what the time is? Nearly half past three!' Terry was unmistakably annoyed.

'I know, I know- that's why I'm ringing- it's Sandra- oh, Terry, what's happened? She hasn't come home!'

Terry was instantly wide awake. 'What? Not come home? But where is she?'

'I don't know. She left the house last night about eight o'clock to go to the audition, and hasn't come home! I must have fallen asleep in front of the telly, waiting for her-' Fred's voice broke- 'oh, Terry, Terry- she hasn't come home... .'

Terry tried to collect his thoughts. 'But she left the hall about- well- about nine o'clock, I suppose-' Then he remembered *how* Sandra had left. 'Oh- she was a bit upset-'

'Upset? *Upset*? What happened?' Fred's voice became angry and suspicious. 'Why was she upset? 'What did you say to her?'

Terry did not quite know how to tell Fred the outcome of Sandra's audition.

'Well- actually, she made a bit of a hash of her song,' he confessed, 'couldn't cope with the top notes. . . she rushed out in quite a state-'

Fred was beside himself with anger. 'And you let her go like that? Didn't anyone go after her?'

'Someone- Sheila Allen, I think- tried to catch her up, but she jumped into her car and drove off. Oh, Fred- I'm so sorry-'

'Oh, my God, where can she be?' Fred was desperate. 'She may have had an accident- any thing- She didn't want to go to the audition, but I made her- Oh God-'

'Calm down, Fred- now, pull yourself together, and let's think what to do. Is there a friend she might have gone to- or a neighbour?'

'She wouldn't have done that- she'd have come home to me.' Fred was adamant, then suddenly an awful thought struck him. 'She got the part, didn't she?'

'No, Fred,' said Terry quietly.

Fred could not take this in. 'What? But she always- Did she know that?'

'Not in so many words,' said Terry, 'But she must have-'

Oh, poor, poor Sandra . .. she must be completely devastated......' Fred's heart missed a beat. 'She might have done something desperate- anything-'

At that moment he heard the sound of the front door opening, then quietly closing.

'Wait a bit, Terry,' said Fred, then called, 'Sandra? Is that you, love? Terry, she's here! She's here! I'll speak to you tomorrow,' and he slammed down the receiver.

Sandra came slowly into the room, weary, bedraggled, her mascara running down her face, and looking every bit her age. She stumbled into Fred's arms. He held her tightly for several minutes, his relief so overwhelming that he was unable to speak. At last he said, 'Oh, Sandra, love- wherever have you been? Are you all right?'

'Yes, I'm all right. . . as right as I'll ever be . . .' she replied dully.

'But where have you been since nine o'clock last night'?' asked Fred gently.

'Oh. . . . driving around. I went up on to Boddington Downs, drove up to that viewpoint where you can see right across the river. It was so peaceful- there was a full moon, and its reflection was making a path across the water . . . . I wished I could walk over it to the other side and never come back. . just simply disappear. I must have sat there for hours, thinking about everything. . . Then I dozed off, and woke up cold and shivering.'

Fred was deeply moved. He gave her a hug, felt how cold she was, and became practical.

'Sit down, love. I'm going to get you a large brandy- you're frozen. Oh, thank God you're all right- I was so worried. I don't know what I'd have done if-' Fred cleared his throat, embarrassed by his unaccustomed emotion.

'Now, where's that brandy?' He busied himself at the cocktail cabinet until he had his feelings under control, poured a brandy for Sandra and one for himself, then sat down beside her. He waited till she had drunk some of her brandy and seemed a little more composed.

'Can you bear to talk about it, love?'

'I'll try, Fred. . . the audition. . . it was just as I feared it would be. I couldn't get anywhere near those top notes- made a complete mess of the song. They even let me have another go- it was worse. I was humiliated- terrified of singing for the first time in my life. Oh, it was horrible, Fred- horrible.' Sandra could not go on.

Fred patted her shoulder gently. 'I know you're terribly upset about the audition- I shouldn't have persuaded you to go. It's my fault- you knew you weren't up to it, and I should have listened. The audition panel might hear you another time, perhaps. . .?'

Sandra shook her head sadly. 'No, Fred. There won't be another time. I'm finished. I shan't sing again. I'm finished.'

Fred sat with his head in his hands. This was his Sandra, the star of every Marleigh show, whom he had watched, entranced, at every performance. It couldn't be ended. How could she give up? She must go on, had to go on.

'Look, love. . .' . . Fred took his wife's hand. 'Perhaps you shouldn't play Mabel- we know it's a terribly taxing role and requires unusual vocal agility which- maybe- doesn't come so easy as we get a bit older-' Sandra tried to interrupt, but Fred went on. 'But next year there's sure to be a show that's right for you- and you'll be back up there where you belong- you'll see.' Sandra was adamant.

'No, Fred. No more shows for me. If it hadn't been for this year's choice of 'Pirates' I might have gone blindly on, not realising that it was time to look at myself and recognise the truth.'

Sandra was on the verge of tears, but she fought them back. 'Oh, most people would wonder what all the fuss is about. It's only a small town operatic society, and what am I? An amateur singer, tasting what passes for stardom for one week in the year.'

'But, love-' Fred tried to intervene, but Sandra went on.

'All our married life I've set my sights on that, to the exclusion of everything else.'

'That's not true, Sandra,' Fred put his arm round his wife, but she shrugged it off, and stood up, confronting him.

'You wanted a family, Fred- you longed for children. But I kept putting it off. 'Oh, let's wait, Fred,' I'd say. 'Let's see what the next show's going to be- it'll probably be something I don't want to do, then we'll start a family.' I promised you that every year, but it never happened. Each time a new show came round I was desperate to play the lead. The idea of children gradually receded into the distance. And you, dear Fred, gave up the idea and encouraged me- basking in the reflected glory of your stage-struck wife. And now. . . no family. . . no glory. What have we got left, Fred? Nothing.'

Fred could not bear Sandra's distress, and was fast becoming as upset as his wife.

'Don't say that, Sandra, love. We've got such a lot- a nice home, we go for wonderful holidays. . . I've got a good job. . . And we've got each other. Who wants a family?'

'You did, Fred. You did. And now it's too late. I'm fifty. And I'm a failure.'

'Don't say that, Sandra, love, don't say that. You know I think the world of you. Doesn't that mean anything?'

But Sandra did not reply. Her extreme pallor emphasised the dark shadows beneath her eyes, and she was still shivering slightly. She seemed to be struggling to speak, but unable to get the words out. Finally, with a great effort, she seemed to pull herself together, and took a deep breath.

'There's something I've never told you, Fred, and now I feel I must. I've kept it to myself so long, and I can't bear it any longer. What you'll think of me, I don't know. It's so terrible that it could end our marriage- that's up to you. I wouldn't blame you if you walked out of that door tonight- or asked *me* to -'

'Oh, Sandra, Sandra,' soothed Fred, 'There's nothing I don't know about you- or anything that would change the way I feel . . . You're overwrought. . . you've had an awful experience, and don't know what you're saying. . . I'll always be here for you, always. . . '

Fred was lost for words. He was not used to such emotional exchanges, and ill-equipped to express his true feelings.

'Do you remember our production of My Fair Lady?'

'Remember it?' Fred smiled. This was better, now they were on safer ground. 'I should think I do. You were the most wonderful Eliza- I said at the time you could have walked straight on to the west end stage. Everyone said so-'

'Never mind my performance. I wonder if you can remember that I went away for a weekend during the early rehearsal period-'

Fred's brow was furrowed. He could not imagine where this conversation was leading, but decided the best thing to do was to play along with Sandra in her present disturbed state.

'It's a long time ago, Sandra . . . But let me see. . . yes. . . it's coming back. Didn't you go to visit that old school friend in Wales? Yes, now I can remember. I couldn't contact you because you spent the weekend in her remote cottage, and there was no phone. . . it was the first time we'd ever been apart since our wedding. And now I come to think of it, I don't believe you had a very good time- weren't you a bit off-colour when you came back?'

'Yes, Fred, I was. And I had not been to stay with an old friend.'

Fred could not see what this disclosure signified, but he sensed something rather ominous in the atmosphere, something that made him uneasy. His voice was unsteady. 'What are you trying to tell me, Sandra?'

'When I knew I was to play Eliza, I was in seventh heaven. I could think of nothing else. Then, about three months into re-hearsal, disaster struck. I was pregnant.'

After Fred's sudden intake of breath, the silence which followed seemed endless. At last he spoke, in a voice that she had never heard before. 'And?'

'I did not go to Wales. I spent that weekend in a clinic in London, having the pregnancy terminated.'

Sandra sat down wearily in a chair by the piano, the other side of the room.

'What?' Fred's voice broke on the word. 'You... *killed. ..our child*?'

He could not speak, he was too deeply affected by this revela-tion. His chest heaved, and his shattered feelings welled up into several piteous sobs.

Sandra turned towards him, but he would not meet her eyes. She had expected her husband to be shocked- upset- at her confes-sion, but was not prepared for the uncontrolled distress she was witnessing. Fred was always so calm, so unruffled by anything fate threw at him. Occasionally she had felt she would like to shake him out of his customary placidity, but now all she longed for was the love and comfort he had unstintingly given her throughout all their years together.

'Fred . . .' she began tentatively, and he raised his head and looked at her as if she were a complete stranger. His eyes were cold and expressionless, his face ashen.

'Go to bed, Sandra,' was all he said.

CHAPTER 8

Maison Terry was, as usual, bustling with activity. Clients in pale mauve gowns relaxed in various stages of coiffure creation, attended by smart young stylists in elegant pale mauve outfits, or being shampooed by juniors in pale mauve overalls. Every garment was embellished with the name 'Maison Terry', embroidered in a darker shade of the same colour. Pristine white net curtains screened the windows, looped back here and there with pale mauve bows, and several ornate gilt mirrors placed in strategic positions reflected vases of artificial purple lilac. There was no doubt about Terry's favourite colour- it was everywhere- and his clients loved it.

He was highly skilled in the art of customer relations; no matter how busy the salon was, Terry always found time to exchange a word with each client- a compliment here, an enquiry about the family there- every one of Terry's clients was made to feel wanted and valued. And they came back again and again.

Eileen was having the finishing touches put to her coiffure. There had been no opportunity to discuss the events of the evening before as yet, but Terry had promised he would make time for a brief chat before Eileen's visit to Sandra.

'This colour really suits you, Eileen,' he said, flicking a recalcitrant curl into place with the tail of his comb.

'Yes, it is rather an attractive shade,' replied Eileen, turning her head to assess the full effect. 'What did you say it was called?'

'Let's see. . . ah- 'Breathless Beige'- I'll make a note of it for next time.' Head on one side, he stood back and viewed his handiwork. 'Shall I bring it forward more at the sides?'

'Yes, do,' said Eileen. 'Oh, that's really very nice.'

'Lacquer, dear?' asked Terry, can poised.

'Just a little, thank you. That's lovely, Terry,' said Eileen, surveying the back view in the proffered mirror.

Terry whisked off her gown. 'Well, there we are,' he said, 'You look very elegant. Now, Eileen, I've put my next client in the hands of my head stylist- she has an unexpected cancellation. The lady won't mind, it's just a blow dry, and Kim's done her hair several times before. So that means we can have twenty minutes or so in my office to see what we can do about Sandra- and do you know, my dear, I've had a really good idea.' Ushering Eileen towards the back of the salon, he called 'Coffee for two, Debbie,' to one of the juniors, and showed Eileen into his small but very chic office, decorated and furnished in his favourite shade.

'What an attractive room, Terry!' remarked Eileen, 'I've never been in your inner sanctum before.'

'Sit down, Eileen- make yourself comfortable, do, and let's see what can be done.' A tray of coffee arrived as he spoke. Terry passed a cup to Eileen and proffered a plate of shortbread fingers.

'I shouldn't really,' said Eileen, but she took one just the same, and the two of them settled down to tackle the awkward problem that lay before them.

'What's this idea of yours, then?' she asked, stirring her coffee thoughtfully.

'I couldn't get back to sleep after that dreadful phone call from Fred at three-thirty am,' said Terry. 'So I got up and made a cup of tea, took it back to bed and just lay there wondering what on earth we could do about Sandra. It's not as if she's played the odd leading part- she's always ruled supreme in the society, and to be toppled from that pinnacle at a stroke- well, it's too unkind.'

'I know,' said Eileen, a worried frown on her face. 'And she was so upset after all the splendid singing she's done for us over the years, it was terrible to see her go to pieces like that- really terrible-' And Eileen shuddered as she relived those few painful moments.

'It would be such a waste if all Sandra's experience were to be lost,' said Terry.

Then, what?' said Eileen. 'What else can she do?'

'Coach.' This was Terry's monosyllabic reply.

'*Coach*?' said Eileen in surprise. 'Who? How?'

'The principals,' said Terry. 'I'm going to be unusually busy with
this production, re-creating it in the twenties, teaching the girls
to do the Charleston, introducing incidental characters for the
older members- oh, there are endless things I don't normally
have to contend with-'

'I see. . . ' said Eileen doubtfully, 'But do you think Sandra would
consider doing it? Teaching someone else to do her part, the
moves and gestures she's always done. . . Wouldn't it be a painful process?'

'I don't know,' replied Terry. 'What I do know is that young Sue
will need all the help she can get, and who better to provide it
than Sandra? If we could persuade her, it would be by far the
best thing for her- much, much better than cutting herself off
from the society and sinking into a deep depression- which I'm
sure she would do.'

'Yes, I think she would,' said Eileen, 'It's been a major part of her
life for so long.'

'And she could work on the trios, too- those marvellous ones
in Act II, with Frederic, Ruth and the Pirate King-' Terry's eyes
shone as he unveiled his plan. 'I would be quite happy to delegate quite a chunk of the principal work to her- I'm sure we'd
see eye to eye- we always have.'

'That's very generous of you, Terry. Not many directors would
be prepared to let someone else play such a large part in the
production process-'

'Nor would I, in the normal course of events,' said Terry. 'But
Sandra's not just someone else- she's an accomplished performer
who's worked under my direction for a number of years. She
knows what I want- my style- the way I see things- and she can
add her own input, born of all those years of experience. What
we must not do, Eileen, is to let her think we are suggesting
this out of pity, resulting from the unfortunate outcome of her

audition. You'll have to tread very carefully when you put this proposition to her.'

'Yes,' replied Eileen, who was not looking forward to the prospect. 'Do you think I can go ahead without consulting the other members of the committee?'

Terry considered for a moment. 'Oh, yes- in these circumstances, I do. You might phone round tonight if Sandra agrees to our idea, but I'm quite sure there's not one member who won't be thrilled if she accepts.'

'You're right,' said Eileen. 'And after all, you are the only one it would really affect. I'd better go round and see her now.' Eileen put her coffee cup back on the tray and rose to go. 'Oh, Terry- my bill-'

'At the desk, dear- I must get a move on now- my next client's due any minute.'

'You've been such a help,' said Eileen, as they returned to the salon. 'I'll give you a ring tonight.'

'Do that, Eileen- good luck- and 'bye for now,' and Terry swept away to attend to his next appointment. As Eileen went to pay her bill, a large elegantly-dressed woman billowed past.

'This way, Mrs Fenwick,' she heard Terry calling. 'My- it *has* grown, hasn't it? Let's see what we can do.'

Eileen smiled as she left the salon. But the smile soon faded as she contemplated her next move. Her task would not be easy.

Marleigh was a pleasant small market town, with a central square dominated by the imposing parish church, at this time of the year surrounded by masses of golden daffodils. Small shops and boutiques filled the rest of the square, together with one or two cafes, notably the Copper Kettle Tearooms- a favourite haunt of Eileen, Sandra and Norma. Many was the occasion they had met there to discuss operatic matters over a pot of tea and a toasted teacake, and many a dilemma had been sorted out there to their satisfaction. Today, however, Eileen hurried past, one sole objective in her mind. Four narrow streets led out of the square, and Eileen hurried down the nearest, turning left at one of the town's two supermarkets, bound for the car park located behind it. Whereas she and Desmond lived in a Victorian terraced house to the west of the town centre, Sandra and Fred had opted for an 'executive detached' in a 'sought after' enclave on the other side of the river. This was not to Eileen's taste at all, for she preferred a house with character, and was constantly searching for contemporary bits and pieces to add to her collection of Victoriana.

Eileen got into her car and was soon on the way- albeit rather reluctantly- to fulfil her task. She negotiated her way round the square, turned right at the traffic lights, and crossed the river by way of the mediaeval bridge, the water meadows on each side looking fresh and spring-like in the bright afternoon sunshine. Eileen looked at her watch: it was nearly two-thirty, and she hoped Sandra would be in. Perhaps she should have phoned. In fact, earlier that morning she had picked up the receiver several times to dial Sandra's number, but each time she had replaced it, not really knowing what to say. She had eventually decided that a face-to-face meeting would be the best thing, and that in any case she must speak to Terry before any interview.

Eileen slowed down as she came to Sandra's turning, and entered the cul-de-sac where the house was situated. She was probably in, Eileen assumed, for her car was parked in the drive. The moment had come, and there was now no alternative but to confront her and make an effort to deal with the sensitive situation. Getting out of her car, Eileen walked up the path and rang the bell.

Nothing happened for a few minutes. Eileen was sorely tempted to beat a hasty retreat, then she noticed the net curtain twitch at Sandra's living room window, and seconds later the front door opened slowly.

Eileen could hardly believe what she saw. The bedraggled figure who stood before her, still in a dressing gown, scarcely resembled the Sandra she knew so well. Her hair, uncombed, hung limply round her face which, utterly devoid of her usual skilful make-up, betrayed her age cruelly. Her eyes were swollen, as if she had been crying, and their expression of hopelessness went straight to Eileen's heart. 'You'd better come in,' said Sandra, and Eileen followed her into the living room.

'Oh, Sandra- Sandra,' said Eileen, and she put her arms round her friend and hugged her. 'Come on, now- things aren't as bad as all that-'

'Oh, but they are,' sobbed Sandra. 'They *are*- You don't know, Eileen- you don't *know*- you don't understand. .. how can you?'

'Why? You're upset because you failed the audition, aren't you? It's not the end of the world, you know,' said Eileen comfortingly.

'I wish it was just that,' said Sandra. 'Oh, how I wish it was. . . But it's worse, much worse. . . I'm finished. . . ' And she burst into another paroxysm of wild sobbing.

'Now, sit down, Sandra,' said Eileen. 'I'm going to make us both a cup of tea. Then you must tell me what's upsetting you so, you really must. Because I've got something interesting to tell you, too, when you feel able to hear it.'

And Eileen went off to put the kettle on, wondering whatever could be causing Sandra such distress. When she returned with the tray of tea, Sandra was slumped in an armchair, but she took the cup Eileen offered, and drank gratefully.

Eileen waited until she seemed a little calmer before trying to find out what was troubling her so. Surely the fact that she was not to play her usual leading role in the forthcoming production could not have plunged her in this dark abyss of despair? Of course she would be upset at having made such a mess of her audition and her failure would be a tremendous blow to her pride, but this display of uncontrolled grief must be due to something more serious. Eileen waited until she was able to speak.

At last Sandra put her cup down and turned to face her. 'It's Fred,' she said. 'He's gone.'

'Gone?' exclaimed Eileen in absolute disbelief. 'Gone? What on earth do you mean? Where? How long for? Sandra, what are you saying?'

'I don't know where,' sobbed Sandra. 'And I don't know how long for. He's gone, that's all I know. . . '

'When did he go?' asked Eileen. 'Now, try to pull yourself together- I want to help you-'

'No-one can help, no-one-' Sandra put her ravaged face in her hands. 'He must have gone early this morning . . . . left a note saying he needed some time to himself- he'd phone in sick to the office, and would be away for a while-'

'For a while?' said Eileen. 'Then he'll be back, Sandra, you mustn't distress yourself like this.' Then she had a sudden thought. 'You're surely not trying to tell me that he's angry with you for not getting the part? That he's gone away to punish you? Oh no- not Fred!'

'No, oh no-' said Sandra- 'Oh, if it were only that! Eileen, oh Eileen- I've been so wicked and selfish- I wouldn't blame Fred if he never came back- I deserve everything that happens to me! If you only knew, Eileen- if you only knew!'

This was more serious than Eileen had anticipated. 'Don't you think you'd better tell me, Sandra? I can't help you unless you explain the circumstances.'

'I don't know how to begin,' said Sandra, pulling a crumpled handkerchief from her pocket and dabbing her eyes. 'It's just too terrible. And nobody else must ever know- Eileen, do you promise me that?'

'Of course I do,' Eileen reassured her. 'And you needn't worry about Desmond- he's the very last person I would ever tell anything in the least confidential.' She smiled encouragingly at Sandra as she said this, and was rewarded by the faint glimmer of a smile in return.

Sandra took a deep breath and started to speak. It was obviously a great effort. She poured out to Eileen all that she had confessed to Fred much earlier that morning, sparing nothing. Eileen sat stunned. She could not believe what she was hearing. When Sandra's sad tale ended, she sat in silence for several minutes.

At last she spoke. 'You mean that playing Eliza in 'My Fair Lady' meant more to you than . . . . than . . . a *child*?' she said at last.

Sandra nodded dumbly. She sat with head bowed, slumped in her chair, a pitiful figure, unrecognisable as the confident well-groomed Sandra that Eileen knew so well.

'It was unforgivable, cruel- oh, yes- I realise it now. I thought we'd have a family later. .. but we never did. . .' Sandra's voice tailed away.

Eileen sat, deep in thought for several minutes.

'Look, Sandra- what's done is done. You've no doubt tortured yourself about this for years- probably every year when the time comes to do our next show it all comes back to you afresh. And now, because of the circumstances of your audition, you felt you had to tell Fred. I think that was very brave. -'

Sandra began to sob again, but this time in a less hysterical way. Eileen got up and went to her, sitting on the arm of her chair.

'Now, Sandra- Fred is shocked, of course he is, and has to come to terms with what you've told him. He needs time to work things out. But he adores you- he's not going to walk out on a marriage which has been so happy for so long. He'll forgive you, of course he will- and even respect you for having had the courage to tell him. After all, you needn't have- you could have gone on living with this secret for the rest of your life. But you didn't. You told him. That was brave, and Fred will realise that.'

'Oh, Eileen, do you really think so?' Sandra raised a tear-stained face to her friend, the faintest dawn of hope in her eyes.

'I do,' replied Eileen, giving Sandra a hug.

'But what shall I do with myself? No rehearsals, no excitement, nothing-'

'I've a suggestion to make,' said Eileen warily, not knowing how Sandra would react. 'From Terry, actually. Would you consider coaching- helping him with the production- being assistant director, in fact?' .

Sandra looked up in surprise. 'Coach? *Me*? Assistant director. . .well, I don't know. . . Why does Terry need one?' she added suspiciously.

Eileen explained what she and Terry had discussed, and how he would have so much more than usual to contend with in such an innovative production.

Sandra looked doubtful. Then she asked, 'Who's going to play Mabel?'

Eileen knew this question must come, and had dreaded it.

'Sue Hebden' she answered. 'And she'll need all the help she can get from an experienced actress like yourself. She's done nothing, and has everything to learn. Oh, Sandra- won't you consider it? Then when Fred comes back- and he will come back- he won't find you moping and miserable. He'll find his attractive wife waiting to welcome him back, busy and cheerful. What do you say?'

Sandra considered. 'I'll think about it.' Eileen knew she must leave the matter for the moment. But she was hopeful.

'Right,' she said cheerfully. 'Now let's have some more tea.'

CHAPTER 9

Julia Hebden and her daughter Sue had just finished their evening meal. Relaxing comfortably at the big pine table in the kitchen, they had reached the coffee stage, and were chatting in a desultory manner about various happenings at work and in the town. Sitting down to a leisurely meal together was a treat for both of them. Although Sue worked normal office hours, her mother was a sister at Marleigh hospital, and her schedule seldom coincided with that of her daughter. Even at weekends Julia was often working, so Sue had always made a point of getting involved in plenty of social activities, and consequently had a wide circle of friends. But this was one of the rare occasions when their leisure time coincided, and each appreciated the chance to catch up on the other's activities.

The kitchen was warm and cosy. Blue and white china gleamed on an old pine dresser which stood in one corner, and plants flourished on the window sill. It was a pleasant place to eat, usually preferred to the more formal dining room. The house was fairly small, but being Edwardian had well proportioned rooms, and many attractive original features, much appreciated by Julia and her daughter. The garden faced south, and although not very large, had a sheltered terrace with a sunny aspect, where the two of them would eat or entertain friends in the summer.

Just over three years ago, Julia and Sue had moved to Marleigh from a small town in Warwickshire. After the tragic motorway accident in which Julia's husband Alan had been killed, neither of them could bear to remain where there were so many memories. They had tried to resume their lives, but found it too difficult, and eventually decided that a complete change of scene was the only course. Many excursions were made to investigate various possible new locations where they might make a fresh start, and they had eventually come upon the busy market town of Marleigh. Julia and Sue had liked it immediately. Enquiries about work prospects proved bright, so they set to work to look for a suitable house, having already received an offer for their own.

They collected a list of suitable properties from one of the estate agents in the square, and exploring Marleigh, discovered number three Croft Terrace. They loved it at first sight, and three months later collected the keys and moved in. Things began to look up for them, and although Alan was never far from their minds, Julia and Sue settled down quickly to their new lives. Julia, a qualified midwife, was soon working at the local hospital, and not long afterwards Sue found a secretarial appointment at a solicitor's office just off the Square.

Before Julia was married, she had been an enthusiastic member of her local operatic society, and had played many leading roles in their productions. She had, in fact, studied singing with a well-known operatic soprano, travelling up to London every week for lessons.. Julia showed great promise, and it was hoped that she might become a professional singer, but marriage had intervened. Alan had by no means discouraged her from pursuing her career, but then Sue had arrived on the scene. Julia decided that a life spent travelling about would not be to her small daughter's advantage, so, after much heart-searching, decided to give it up, and when her daughter reached school age, embarked on a career in nursing. Sue had obviously inherited her mother's vocal talent, and Julia had encouraged her, persuading her to take singing lessons. Discovering that there was a well established operatic society in Marleigh, Julia suggested that her daughter might join. This, of course, she had done, and was enjoying it enormously so far. Meeting Ian, to whom she had been instantly attracted, was a decided bonus.

'More coffee?' asked Julia. 'There's plenty left in the pot.'

Yes, thanks,' said Sue, passing her cup. 'What are we going to do this evening- any plans?'

'Aren't you going out? It's Saturday night, after all,' said her mother. 'You should be enjoying yourself-not sitting at home with me.'

'It's ages since I had a night in,' observed Sue. 'It's a nice change. And I'm out nearly every evening next week. I used to be free on Tuesdays, then you made me join the operatic society. Nearer the production week it will be Thursdays as well. Then the last two weekends we apparently have to rehearse on Sundays- is that what they usually do?'

'Oh, yes,' replied her mother. 'We always did.' Then a sudden thought occurred to her. 'Hey, Sue- isn't it tonight that you can phone- who is it- Eileen- to find out the result of the auditions?'

'Oh, yes- so it is,' said Sue. 'But there's really no point. Sandra is the leading lady of Marleigh Operatic Society, has been for years, and no doubt will continue to be for the foreseeable future. I just went along to the audition for fun, really-'

'But you said there was some drama at the end, didn't you? Some story about Sandra rushing out in a fury- what was all that about?'

'Oh, goodness knows- she must have had some disagreement with someone or other. I'm sure it's all settled now.'

'She can't go on playing juveniles for ever,' observed Julia. 'And *I* certainly shouldn't dream of playing Mabel, though actually I'm probably younger that Sandra.'

'I'm sure you are,' said Sue, regarding her mother affectionately. 'And much more attractive, too.'

It was true. Julia, at forty-seven, was as slim as her daughter, and her complexion had remained as youthful as her figure. The few faint lines at the corner of her eyes were almost invisible in the mellow light of the table lamp. Sue suddenly felt an overwhelming sense of admiration and love for her mother, who had coped with the tragedy of Alan's death, the upheaval of the move to Marleigh, the challenges of a new job- and still managed to hold on to her zest for life, and all it had to offer. Most important of all, she had retained the irrepressible sense of humour that they both shared.

The auditions were still on Julia's mind. 'Well, if not Mabel, you might get one of the small parts- they're quite fun to play- why not call Eileen and find out?'

Sue still looked doubtful, but gave in. Just as she was about to get up from her chair, the phone rang in the hall.

'I'll go,' she said. 'But it's probably for you. Are you in or out?'

Julia laughed. 'Depends who it is,' she said, and began to clear the table.

In a few moments Sue came back into the room. Her eyes were shining, and she looked somewhat bemused.

'That was Ian,' she said. 'He's just been on to Eileen. He says *I've* been cast as Mabel.' Julia shrieked with delight, and hugged her daughter rapturously. 'I knew it, I knew it!' she said, 'I just *knew* it!'

Sue looked decidedly shaken. 'Can I do it?' she asked.

'*Do* it?' exclaimed Julia, 'I should just think you can!' And the two of them, singing Mabel's song, 'Poor Wand'ring One' at the top of their voices, grabbed each other round the waist and broke into a mad waltz routine, which came to an untimely end when they collided with the waste bin and collapsed into a couple of chairs.

'Hey!' panted Sue, 'Ian said he'd call round and take me for a celebration drink in about ten minutes- 'I'd better change into something decent.'

She surveyed the half-cleared table. 'Shall I help you with this first?'

'Good heavens, no,' said Julia, trying to get her breath back. 'Prima donnas don't do menial work! Most of this'll go in the dishwasher anyway- off you go, and get changed.'

'OK, I'd better- can't go out like this.' And Sue, in her shabby old jeans and baggy tee shirt, disappeared to effect a lightning transformation.

No sooner had Julia cleared the table than the doorbell rang, and she hastened to answer it. On the step stood a tall young man. For a few moments they regarded each other with interest, and each liked what they saw.

'Ian?' said Julia. 'Come in- Sue won't be a minute.' She took Ian into the sitting room. 'Do sit down,' she said. 'I'm Julia- Sue's mother.'

'Hi,' said Ian. 'I'd have guessed that- you're so like her. But you're more like her sister- you don't look much older-'

Julia laughed. 'You can come again! What a compliment!'

'I mean it,' said Ian. 'But what do you think of the news? Isn't it brilliant?'

Julia sat down on a small chair opposite Ian. 'It was so unexpected. Sue was convinced that Sandra would get the leading role, as always. What do you think has happened?'

Ian shrugged his shoulders. 'Can't imagine. There must have been some sort of row when she went in to her audition- that's all we know. No doubt we'll find out.'

'Can I offer you a drink?' asked Julia.

'Better not- driving,' replied Ian. 'I'll have a half in the pub- that's all I allow myself- unless I decide to walk, that is. But I couldn't let this occasion pass without a celebration drink. Won't you join us?'

'Not this evening, thanks all the same. Another time- that would be lovely.'

Ian looked round the room, and his gaze lighted on a small upright piano in one corner. 'Who plays?' he asked.

'I do,' said Julia. 'I often accompany Sue when she has something to learn. J hoped to be a professional singer years ago, but things got in the way. Nice things,' she added, with a smile. 'Such as Sue's arrival on the scene!'

'I see,' said Ian. 'So she has her own vocal coach- no wonder she knocked 'em for six at her audition! '

They both laughed, comfortably at ease with each other, then Sue appeared in the doorway, looking attractive in clean jeans and a raspberry pink sweat shirt. She had put on a touch of make-up, but it was not that which had put the sparkle in her eyes, but the exhilaration of the unexpected news, and the exciting prospect which lay before her.

'Hi, Ian! Where are we going then? I was just about to have a quiet night in when you called.'

'Sorry about that,' laughed Ian. 'But I think we must mark this
occasion with a toast to your success. I've asked your mother to
join us, but she said perhaps another time.' 'Oh, she's up at crack
of dawn tomorrow, aren't you, Mum?' said Sue. 'The NHS is
relentless.'

Ian looked puzzled, then Julia explained. 'I work at the hospital,
and tomorrow I'm on early. Now off you go and enjoy yourselves.'

'Well, if you're sure,' said Ian. We'll be on our way, and leave you
in peace.'

Sue kissed her mother. 'Don't wait up,' she said, 'Though I shan't
be late.'

Julia stood at the front door as the pair made their way to Ian's
car.

'Goodbye, Mrs Hebden-' Ian called.

'*Julia-*' insisted Sue's mother.

'Julia it is,' agreed Ian, and with a last wave, he started up the
car. 'Now, which hostelry shall we make for?'

'Everywhere's a bit crowded on a Saturday night,' said Sue. 'But
why not try the Coach and Horses- it's a bit off the beaten track.
Anywhere but the Marleigh Arms- we shall see enough of that
place in the next few months!'

'You're telling me,' said Ian. 'OK- the Coach and Horses it is.'

A few minutes later they had arrived, and were soon ensconced
with their drinks at a corner table, conveniently vacated just as
they entered the bar. Ian raised his glass.

'Congratulations!' he said. 'How you ousted Sandra from her
non-assailable position remains a mystery.'

'Oh, it was just pure talent!' said Sue. 'They had no other option.
Seriously, though- I was completely stunned when you told me.,
Whatever will Sandra do? She'll hate me, I'm sure- a newcomer,
still wet behind the ears, stepping straight into the plum principal role- her role. I shall feel very awkward when I meet her.'

'It won't be easy,' admitted Ian. 'But I shouldn't think we'll see much of her- she wouldn't play one of the small parts, and on no account would she be in the chorus. I think she'll stay away- certainly for the time being.'

'Oh, Ian- with all this excitement, I've never asked how *you* got on! You're not playing Frederic by any chance?'

'Not a hope,' said Ian. 'Oh no, it's Samuel for me- the Pirate King's sidekick, just as I expected. I'm afraid it's old Ron you'll have to play those love scenes with!'

'Ugh! I'm not looking forward to that,' said Sue, with a grimace. 'And how can he possibly masquerade as a twenty-one year old- it's outrageous!'

'I suppose it is,' laughed Ian. 'And you'll have to be on your guard, Sue. Ron's quite likely to take advantage of what he'll consider your lack of stage experience. He may try to upstage you, or hang on to high notes in the duets much longer than you do- that sort of thing.'

'But that's terrible,' said Sue indignantly. 'How did Sandra manage?'

'Oh, she knew just how to deal with him. After all, they'd worked together for years. She gave as good as she got, and many's the time Ron's got a sharp dig in the ribs or a high heel jabbed into his foot to make him come off a particularly long top note. Sandra was very accomplished at that sort of thing, and would administer the treatment quite imperceptibly, and with the sweetest smile on her face. You'll have to acquire the same technique!'

'I don't really want to,' said Sue. 'How can you lose yourself in your character and play a tender love scene if you're constantly aware of a battle of wills between you and your lover?'

Ian laughed. 'I don't really mean to say that Ron's an intentionally mean person, Sue- it's just that when he's on stage, he only thinks about himself, and the impression he's creating upon the audience. He just can't help it- he's had it easy for too long-'

'Well, I may be inexperienced, but I'm a quick learner,' said Sue darkly, 'and he'll soon find out I'm no pushover- I'll show him!'

'I bet you will,' said Ian. 'But I don't think you'll have much of a problem. When the audience see a young and attractive Mabel appearing on the scene, they won't have much interest in her somewhat elderly suitor- in fact, he'll be more like your father than your would-be lover! No, I don't mean that- that's too cruel. Ron really does sing well in spite of his advancing years, and he's got quite a following locally.'

'We-ell' said Sue reluctantly, 'I'll try and get on with him, for the good of the show, but it won't be easy. Oh, I wish it was *you* playing Frederic, Ian we- could have fun.'

'Yes. But I tell you what,' said Ian, as an idea struck him, 'I could give you a hand with learning your part. Your mother plays the piano, doesn't she? We could have a go at those duets- would that be a help?'

'Oh, yes,' replied Sue. 'That'd be marvellous. Turning up at rehearsal knowing what I'm doing would give me a lot of confidence- would you really?'

'Of course,' said Ian. 'Consider it a deal.'

They clinked glasses and drank to Ian's proposition.

'Now, tell me a bit about the society,' said Sue. 'What's Terry like to work with? D'you think he's a good director?'

Ian considered carefully. 'Yes, I do. I know he seems a bit airy-fairy, but when he gets down to the production, he's very efficient. He has everything worked out before rehearsals begin, and knows exactly what he wants.'

'Sounds good,' observed Sue.

'But,' said Ian, 'most important- if you have your own ideas about your character, a move, or a gesture- he'll listen. That's more than you can say for some directors. And if he likes your idea, he'll let you have your way. In other words- he's flexible. And I like that.'

'Well, I look forward to rehearsing with him,' said Sue. 'I shall need all the help I can get. And what about Jack? How do you get on with him?'

'Oh, there's no doubt that he's an excellent musical director,' said Ian with enthusiasm. 'He keeps everything going at a sparkling pace, which is a good thing with amateurs. But I warn you- he's mad keen on diction- always on at us about it. Says there's no point doing Gilbert and Sullivan if you can't hear the words.'

'Well, that's fair enough', said Sue, finishing her glass of wine.

'Would you like another?' asked Ian, but Sue shook her head.

'No, thanks, I don't think so. You know, Ian- on audition night, Sharon and Angie gave me a hard time. Why was that, d'you think? Was it just because I'm new? Are they likely to make things awkward for me when they know I'm going to play Mabel?'

'I shouldn't think so for a minute- there's no harm in those two- in fact, they're usually a lot of fun. But bear in mind, they're great fans of Sandra's, and they'll have to get used to the fact that someone who's just joined the society has- in their eyes- ousted her from her established place as Marleigh's leading lady. This may take some time. You'll just have to be patient, and turn a blind eye- and ear- to any possible unpleasantness. It won't last.'

'I do hope not,' said Sue doubtfully. 'I do want to enjoy my operatic debut!'

'And you will,' promised Ian.

Sue nodded. What's Mike Mitchell like? He seems nice- but do I detect a lack of sincerity? And has he had some sort of quarrel with Sheila Allen? She seemed very cool towards him in the pub- almost rude, in fact.'

Oh, Mike's all right,' said Jan. 'But quite a one for the ladies, so watch out! He and Sheila were very close during the last production- in fact I rather suspected there was something going on between them at one time. But if there was, they were very discreet about it, and whatever happened then seems to have ended now.'

'It's all very interesting,' observed Sue thoughtfully. I suppose there are lots of affaires and intrigues in every society. I expect I'll soon find out what's going on, and who fancies whom.' She burst out laughing. 'One thing's certain- I'm not likely to fall in love with my leading man!'

CHAPTER 10

The clock in Sheila Allen's kitchen struck seven. It was Monday night, and she could look forward to an evening uninterrupted by husband or children. Brian was at his weekly computer class, Emma had gone swimming and was going on to her best friend's house afterwards for some alleged revision, and Matt was at his weekly karate session. Sheila had two hours or more to catch up on all the things that had piled up after the weekend. First on the list was some baking, then a whole pile of ironing. She went to the fridge for the fat, took down the jar of flour from the shelf, filled a measuring jug with cold water, and assembled the various utensils needed. Tying an apron round her waist, she switched on the oven and proceeded to weigh the ingredients into a mixing bowl.

As Sheila began to rub the fat into the flour, her mind wandered over the previous week's events. How strange the auditions had been this year- the delay in announcing the results was odd, for one thing. She had never known an audition evening when the cast list had not been announced at the end, and she had been a member of the society for eight- no, nine years.

Why had Sandra rushed out of the hall in such a state? Was that the reason Eileen had looked so flustered when she came and told them that the results would be delayed? It was all very strange. Sheila had phoned her on Saturday, as had been suggested, and had learned that she had been successful in her bid for the part of Ruth. She was pleased about that, for it would be great fun to play. Ruth, a 'piratical maid of all work' had been Frederic's nursemaid, and had mistakenly apprenticed her young charge to a pirate instead of a pilot, owing-or so she said-to being hard of hearing. Horrified at her mistake, she throws in her lot with the pirate band, and when the curtain rises on Act I Frederic is celebrating what he believes to be his twenty-first birthday. Sheila felt that the role would give her plenty of scope for both acting and singing, and- she admitted to herself- she was relieved that Ruth has no contact with the Major General.

That role was to be played by Mike Mitchell, and Sheila had her reasons for not wishing to be involved with him, reasons which she tried hard to push to the back of her mind.

Most surprising of all was the news that young Sue Hebden was to play Mabel, and not Sandra. Surely Eileen's embarrassment after the auditions must have had something to do with this? Sandra's unaccountable behaviour as she rushed out of the hall was totally out of character- had she been told then and there that she was not to play the leading role? Sue would make a delightful Mabel, Sheila thought, providing she could cope with the difficult vocal demands and obviously she could, or she would not have been cast. It was all very puzzling. Sheila added the water to the bowl, and mixed the pastry deftly with a knife. Turning it out on to the floured board, she began to roll it lightly. Then the front doorbell rang.

'Oh, hell!' said Sheila crossly. 'Who on earth is that? I'm not expecting any callers tonight-' Wiping her hands on a tea towel, she went to the door and opened it. She stood, frozen with shock, when she saw who it was.

'Hello, Sheila,' said Mike Mitchell. 'Aren't you going to ask me in?'

'What are *you* doing here?' she demanded.

'I think we need to talk,' replied Mike. 'And I know you're always alone on a Monday evening, so I thought it would be a good opportunity. May I come in?'

'I suppose you'd better,' said Sheila reluctantly. 'Just for a few minutes- I'm very busy,' and she led Mike into the kitchen.

'I can see you are,' said Mike. 'And you've got flour on your nose.'

Sheila brushed it off crossly, aware that she must look at her most unattractive in an apron, no make-up, and her hair tied back carelessly.

Mike, however, thought she looked rather appealing and strangely youthful, her face flushed from the warmth of the kitchen and her lovely auburn hair untidily screwed up in a childish ponytail.

'You'd better tell me what you want,' said Sheila, 'and then go. I have to get this baking done, and I've lots to do after that.'

Oh, Sheila, Sheila-' said Mike unhappily, 'We can't go on like this.'

'Like what?' Sheila sounded angry. 'We made a bargain, Mike. We *have* to stick to it. More talking will get us nowhere- there is simply no more talking to do.'

Sheila looked at Mike, leaning against the breakfast bar, and her heart seemed to miss a beat. If she did not take a firm grip on herself she would be lost. For she knew suddenly and irrevocably that the old magic was as strong as ever, and the lithe figure, the handsome face with the expressive eyes that promised so much still had the power to destroy her resolve.

'Oh, Mike-' she moaned, and he moved quickly round the table to take her in his arms. They stood together in silence for a few moments, then he put his hand beneath her chin and lifted her face to his. He smoothed back a lock of hair which had escaped from her ponytail, and looked into her eyes.

'See what I mean?' he said.

'Yes,' said Sheila. 'I see exactly what you mean. But there's nothing we can do.'

And she sat down wearily and buried her head in her hands.

'It was all very well when we were just friends, but then our relationship went too far, and that weekend when I had to tell so many lies- well, that should never have happened.'

'Never have *happened*?' Mike was angry. 'Did it mean nothing to you except the inconvenience of making a few excuses to the family? Well- it meant more to me than that!'

'Oh, please don't misunderstand me, Mike- of course it meant more. But I've never lied to Brian before- he trusted me, and never thought of doubting me for one moment- don't you see, that makes it all so much worse?'

Mike turned away, and there was a silence, broken only by the sound of the clock striking eight.

'I want you to leave him,' he said quietly, still with his back towards her.

'*Leave* him?' cried Sheila, aghast. 'And what about the children? What about Emma and Matt? How can you suggest such a thing? And where does your wife come into this?'

'Of course, I should leave Jackie,' said Mike. 'You know there's nothing between us- hasn't been for years. Our relationship is merely platonic- she has her room, and I have mine. The hours we work hardly ever coincide, and we see little of each other. We're friends, of course- there's no friction between us- there's nothing at all, in fact.'

Sheila thought about Jackie- she'd only met her socially, at last night parties after the show, but she'd always seemed pleasant. She was very attractive- slim, and elegant, and Sheila knew that she held down a very important job as personal assistant to the general manager of a large software firm in Oxford. This meant a daily fifteen mile journey to work, and occasional trips abroad with her boss, which meant that Mike was often on his own. Sheila knew that they had wanted a family in the early days of their marriage, but that when Jackie failed to conceive, neither had fancied the idea of extensive tests or the trauma of IVF, and according to Mike they had gradually drifted apart.

'What are you asking me to do, Mike?' said Sheila. She could scarcely comprehend the enormity of what he was suggesting.

'Sheila- it's simple. I love you- I *love* you, and I can't go through the rest of my life without you. And I believe you feel the same- I *know* you feel the same. We've tried avoiding each other, ignoring each other- but it just doesn't work. Can't you see that?' Mike knelt down by Sheila's chair and put his arms round her. She shivered, and he drew her towards him.

'But the children- the children- what would they do without me? How would they cope- they have exams soon, they need my support. And Brian couldn't manage on his own. . . '

A sob caught in Sheila's throat, and Mike drew her close.

'There sometimes comes a time in our lives when we have to make a decision, Sheila. Are you going to spend the rest of your life in boring domesticity? We could travel, explore- there are so many things out there waiting for us. I want you- *need* you- don't say no, darling. . . . don't say no-' he pleaded.

'But, Emma- Matt. . . . I love them, Mike-' Sheila's voice broke as she thought of her children.

'How old are they? Fifteen? Seventeen?' Sheila nodded. 'In a few years they'll be leaving you. And you'll be left with Brian.'

Sheila thought of her husband. Dear, dependable Brian. Always there, kind, reliable, and . . . . dull. Pottering about the house and garden in his baggy old sweaters, always engaged in some DIY project or other. No interest in music, opera or any of the arts. And totally uninspired when it came to love-making. Sheila realised now, after all these years, that even in the early years of their marriage she had never experienced the passion and fulfil- ment she had discovered with Mike. That had been something new and wonderful, something she had never dreamed of. To discover such feelings for the first time at the age of forty-three had been shattering for Sheila. How, she thought confusedly, could she bear to spend the rest of her life with Brian? In her imagination the dreary years stretched out before her: the boring holidays, odd visits to the cinema- occasionally the theatre- the daily routine, seeing Brian off in the morning to his mundane job in a local government department, doing her own part-time sec- retarial job- could she bear it any longer? Common sense told her she must, but a desperate longing to be free, to spread her wings and to go where her heart dictated urged her in the opposite direction. She was torn between the two decisions. Mike sensed that she was weakening, and took advantage of her dilemma.

'Look, Sheila, we're not mad young things rushing into an im- petuous affaire- we're both mature enough to see we've reached a point in our lives when we've recognised that somewhere along the way we've taken a wrong turning. We're both at the mid-life crossroads- and we can see clearly which road to take. It won't be easy, but we can do it.' Mike pulled Sheila to her feet and kissed her very gently. She could not but respond, and their kisses became more and more passionate until she broke away desperately.

'Mike, Mike! We *mustn't*- look at the time- it's nearly nine o'clock, and I've hardly started on the things I have to do- Brian and the children will be back before long- you must go now! There's no more time for talking- oh, please go *now*!'

Sheila was in great distress, and Mike realised he had pushed her far enough. If he could get her alone again, just for an hour or two, he knew he would win her over.

'Listen,' he said. 'Tell Brian you've got an extra rehearsal on Thursday- that's not unusual- and we'll talk about this some-where quiet- out of Marleigh, if you like. There's a music re-hearsal tomorrow- I'll see you there, and we can decide when and where to meet.'

Sheila had not the strength to argue. 'All right,' she said weakly, 'but go now.'

Mike kissed her again. 'Goodnight, darling,' he said softly, and Sheila heard the front door close quietly behind him.

She set to work to finish the job she had begun before Mike's unexpected visit had turned her world upside down. Applying herself to the task of pastry-making was the very last thing she felt like doing, but life had to go on normally for the family- at least for the time being. Automatically she placed a circle of pas-try on a baking dish, filled it with the fruit that she had prepared earlier, covered it with more pastry, trimmed and edged it, then put it in the oven. Her head ached, and the emotionally-charged atmosphere together with the heat of the kitchen made her feel faint. Clearing away the debris, she filled the kettle and switched it on- perhaps a strong cup of coffee would help her to regain some semblance of calm before the family returned.

Sitting at the table and sipping her coffee, Sheila re-lived that momentous evening. Could she really contemplate the devastat-ing upheaval that Mike was proposing? Leave Brian to cope with two teenage children, run the house and do a full-time job- was that an option? Then memories of that weekend with Mike came flooding back- not only the wonder of her sexual awakening, so long denied her- but the companionship and the long talks about all the many things they had in common; the discovery of so many mutual interests- art, theatre, music, and the desire to travel. There was so much to see- so much to do. And she would never see or do anything with Brian. Surely she deserved to *live*?

Sheila thought of Mike, and any obligation to her husband and children receded to the back of her mind. On Thursday she would meet him, and they would discuss their future together. Till then she must remain calm, and try to acquire a veneer of normality. It would not be easy.

CHAPTER 11

Eileen dusted the last of her Staffordshire china dogs and put it back with the others on the mantelpiece. She glanced at the clock. It was ten to eleven- nearly coffee time, and Sandra would soon be here. It was almost a fortnight since Eileen had visited her, and she had phoned the previous evening to ask if she could come round for a chat. She had apparently given a lot of thought to the suggestion that she might be Terry's assistant on the show, and wanted to talk it over once more before making her final decision. Reading between the lines, Eileen guessed that there was more on Sandra's mind than society matters, and was fully prepared to lend a sympathetic ear and help her sort out her problems. Sandra had not mentioned Fred, so Eileen had no idea whether or not he had returned, and if he had, how things were working out.

Hurrying into the kitchen, she switched on the kettle and made ready a tray with cups, saucers and a plate of chocolate digestive biscuits- Sandra's favourites. If she refuses these, thought Eileen, she's still in a really bad way.

As she was pouring the water into the cafetiere, the doorbell rang, and she hurried to answer it.

'Sandra- how good to see you- come in, my dear,' said Eileen, showing her into the sitting room. 'Just put your coat on that chair. Do sit down, and I'll fetch the coffee. It's all ready.'

Eileen carried in the tray and set it down on a small table. Pouring a cup for Sandra, she said, 'Milk, but no sugar- that's right, isn't it? And how about a biscuit? I know you like these.'

To her satisfaction Sandra accepted a chocolate biscuit.

'That's a good sign,' thought Eileen. She sat down with her coffee and waited for her friend to speak.

'Fred's come home,' said Sandra.

'Oh, my dear- I'm so glad- I knew he would. That's wonderful. When did he get back?'

'He was away for a week. I didn't know what to do. I spring-cleaned the house- did all the things I'd meant to do for ages- you know, re-covered some cushions, finished a sweater I'd been knitting since last autumn, painted the shelves in the utility room- anything, just to keep busy and tire myself out so that I could get some sleep at night.' Eileen looked at her friend. There was no doubt that Sandra showed signs of stress and an obvious lack of sleep, for there were dark smudges beneath her eyes, but she had put on her make-up carefully, and her hair, though not as well-groomed as usual, was newly-washed. Eileen sensed an aura of resignation about her. The rather hard, sophisticated Sandra she knew so well had disappeared- temporarily perhaps- giving place to a softer, more vulnerable person.

'But you say Fred's come back? Where had he been? Is everything all right between you?' asked Eileen anxiously.

'Yes, he's back. I don't know where he went- and everything's not all right- not really. I didn't ask any questions, and he didn't volunteer any explanation of his absence, or say where he'd been.'

'But you're on speaking terms, aren't you? You must talk about *something*?'

Eileen was disturbed at Fred's uncharacteristic behaviour- this was not like him at all.

'Oh, we *speak*- Fred's polite, and we pass the time of day. He's been going out most evenings- you know he belongs to the Conservative club- and I'm in bed when he gets back. He's sleeping in the guest room, anyway, and goes off earlier than usual to work in the morning- to avoid seeing me, I suppose. That's how we are now- and *will* be, it seems. And it's all my fault-' Tears came to Sandra's eyes and rolled down her face. She made no effort to check them, and the sight of her friend in such distress touched Eileen's heart.

'Sandra, don't cry- it takes time to get over things. Fred will come round, I have no doubt of that.' Eileen stirred her coffee thoughtfully. 'Give him some space- be friendly towards him, and above all, try to keep cheerful. I know it's not easy in the circumstances, but soon we shall start production rehearsals and if you decide to take on the coaching, you'll be out a lot, too. And Fred will realise that he needs you just as you need him- I know he will. Now, dry those tears and let's talk about the show.' Sandra gave a watery smile, blew her nose, and made an effort to pull herself together.

'Thanks, Eileen. It helps to talk about it. You're a good friend for listening. Now, what's Terry got in mind for me to do? I haven't made a decision about it yet- I'll have to discuss it fully with him of course before I commit myself.'

'Naturally,' said Eileen. 'But it does sound interesting, and I think you could make a marvellous job of it.'

'When do production rehearsals begin?' asked Sandra.

'Let me see,' said Eileen. consulting her diary. 'Music rehearsals go on until the end of April, then the first Tuesday in May is when we start on production, with big chorus numbers in the large hall and principals' scenes in the smaller one-'

Before Eileen could elaborate, the telephone rang in the hall.

'Oh, bother,' she said, putting down her coffee cup. 'I'd better answer it.'

She hurried out of the room, and Sandra heard her say, 'Hello? Oh, that's great- excellent- we'll see you in about five minutes, then.'

'Who was that?' asked Sandra suspiciously as Eileen came back into the room. She had thought they were to have a tete-a-tete. Eileen looked very pleased.

'That was Terry,' she said. 'He's had a last minute cancellation, and he knew you were coming this morning, so he's offered to pop round for ten minutes.'

This news seemed to bother Sandra. She half stood up to go, but Eileen motioned her to stay.

'I'm not sure I'm ready to see anyone else yet,' she said. 'I haven't seen Terry since. .. since that audition.' Sandra shuddered at the memory of it.

'Terry's just the one you *should* see,' said Eileen. 'He's such a sympathetic person underneath that flamboyant exterior- and he's very fond of you, Sandra. If you're seriously thinking you might assist him with the production, well, the schedule will have to be planned, and the longer you avoid meeting anybody from the society, the harder it's going to be.'

Sandra finished her coffee without speaking, and accepted a refill from Eileen. At last she gave a resigned sigh.

'You're right, of course. I'll see what Terry has to say, and whether I think I can cope with the coaching. Teaching someone else to play my part- to take the place I've occupied for so long- well, it's not going to be easy.'

'But you can do it, Sandra,' said Eileen. 'I know you can.'

She glanced out of the window as a car pulled up outside. 'Here's Terry now. I'll let him in, and go and make some more coffee.'

Terry peeped round the door, smiled at Sandra, and held out his arms. With a muffled sob she stood up and rushed into his embrace, and for a few seconds neither spoke. At last Terry held her at arms' length and looked searchingly into her face.

'Poor darling,' he said. 'Poor darling- you've had such a terrible time. But we'll make it right, you'll see. Now, let's sit down and we'll see what we can do.'

Obediently Sandra sat down on a chair facing him, and waited for him to speak.

'You know what this is about, Sandra, Eileen's put you in the picture. And don't think for one minute that I'm suggesting you help me on the production side because I'm sorry for you. I happen to need someone to do individual coaching- block some of the principals' scenes maybe, but above all, to help them with characterisation, moves and gestures. And I want someone who knows what they're doing. Not just anyone. And if you say no, then I shall be really stuck. But I'll have to find *someone*. I'd like that someone to be you. What do you say?'

Why do you need an assistant? You've always done everything yourself- and wonderfully well.' Sandra looked doubtful.

'This show is completely different,' replied Terry. 'Putting it into the twenties has posed all sorts of problems- teaching the girls to Charleston is one of them! And having auditioned and chosen the most suitable ones for General Stanley's daughters, I'm having to introduce some subsidiary characters for the older ladies, and a couple of the chaps. Not speaking parts, of course, but something more acceptable for them to play. All this takes time, and I want to be able to delegate some of the other work to a reliable person. now, is that going to be *you*?'

Sandra pondered on what Terry had said.

'It's going to be difficult to work with another soprano. . . . what's Sue Hebden like? Would she take direction from me? And Ron-whatever would *he* think?'

'Sue's delightful, but has virtually no stage experience. I'm pretty sure she'd soak up direction from you like blotting paper. As for Ron- well, you leave him to me.'

They both laughed at this, and Eileen returned at that moment with reinforcements, pleased to hear Sandra laughing for the first time for weeks.

'And there's another important thing,' said Terry. 'Don't think that because you're not playing Mabel in this show, that you've retired from the stage-'

'What do you mean-' said Sandra, 'Of course I have- isn't it obvious?'

'No, it is not,' replied Terry firmly. 'Mabel should be young- we know that. And she has to be able to sing some stratospheric notes. But think of the parts you could still play- the Widow, for instance. Oh, Sandra, you're not giving up- don't think that for one minute!'

'Oh, if only-' said Sandra wistfully, her eyes lighting up at the prospect.

'There are so many parts that are just *you*, Sandra- only think-' Terry's enthusiasm mounted as he sought to rebuild Sandra's self-confidence.

'What about Rosalinda in 'Die Fledermaus', for instance- she's got some high notes in that Czardas, but nothing you couldn't cope with. And with Sue maybe as Adele- well, there you are! And what about Orpheus's sophisticated mother in 'Orpheus in the Underworld?' Now, *that's* you to a T! I could go on and on . . .'

Well, Sandra,' said Eileen, 'The future looks bright after all, doesn't it?'

The atmosphere in the room had lightened considerably. Eileen looked relieved, Sandra seemed much more cheerful, and Terry was his usual effervescent self. He looked at the clock.

'Heavens, is that the time?' He finished his coffee in one gulp. 'Mrs Josephs will be chafing at the bit! Well, Sandra- is it yes or no?'

Sandra smiled, a smile of genuine pleasure. 'For you, Terry- anything!' she said.

'Wonderful- my day is made! I'll be in touch. Thanks for the coffee, Eileen- must fly!' Terry disappeared with a flourish, and jumping into his car with a wave to Eileen, who was at the front door, accelerated rapidly down the road towards the town square. Eileen closed the door and returned to the sitting room.

'How d'you feel now, Sandra- better?'

'Yes, oh yes-' said Sandra. 'Terry's like a tonic.' She looked thoughtful for a moment. 'I'm determined to make a success of this coaching for his sake and of course for mine. Thank you, Eileen, for all you've done to help me. You've been a real friend.'

She stood up and reached for her coat. 'I'll be on my way now. I'm so glad I came.'

The two women kissed affectionately, and Eileen saw Sandra out, waving as she got into her car. As it disappeared round the corner, she gave a big sigh of relief. It had been a most successful morning.

CHAPTER 12

Sue and Ian sat opposite each other in a small Italian bistro just off Marleigh market place. The music rehearsal that evening had, for them, finished early, for the Sergeant of the Police had been kept behind to go through his song, together with his doughty band of policemen. So, as they were free at nine o'clock Ian had suggested they go for some pasta and a glass or two of wine.

'This is a good idea,' said Sue, sipping her wine with great enjoyment. 'Mum's working this evening, and I only grabbed a sandwich before the rehearsal. I'm starving.'

'Me too. I got home from work late- had to show some clients round a property about six miles out of Marleigh at five thirty, and they took ages, discussing how all their furniture might fit in, what colours they would paint everything, and what they would do to the garden. I thought I'd never make the rehearsal.'

'D'you enjoy working in estate agency?' asked Sue. 'Is it interesting, or can it be boring?'

'Well, all jobs can be boring at times, I suppose,' said Ian. 'But on the whole it's very varied, and you get out and about a lot, which is good- better than sitting in an office all day-'

'Which is what I do, of course,' laughed Sue. 'But I've got a lovely boss. There are only two other girls in the office and we get on terribly well, so I think I'm lucky.' Their pasta arrived just then, and both set to with hearty appetites.

'What a nice little place this is,' observed Sue. '1 haven't been here before. This pasta's delicious.'

'Yes- I often come here,' said Ian. 'When I can't be bothered to cook.'

'Are you a good cook?' asked Sue. 'Do you live alone? I really know very little about you!'

'Yes, 'I'm not bad at all,' replied Ian. 'And I do live alone. . .now.'

As he spoke, his expression became rather pensive, but he did not elaborate on his statement, and Sue felt she could not pursue the matter. Obviously there was a sad story here. Probably he would tell her about it some day when they had known each other longer. They were, after all, fairly new acquaintances. Ian was tall, slim, and though not exactly handsome in the conventional sense, his ready smile and easy manner were very appealing. More important, Sue decided, he was great fun, and very good company. And it was useful to have a friend in the society who could advise her how to avoid any tricky situations that arose.

'You sang well tonight,' said Ian. 'You opened a few people's eyes, and gave Angie and Sharon quite a shock.'

'Well, I've broken the ice. It was slightly nerve-wracking having to sing in front of the society for the first time, knowing that most people were thinking that I was usurping Sandra's rightful place. But I've done it now, and quite a few paid me some very nice compliments as we were leaving.'

'I should think so. They don't know how lucky they are,' said Ian. 'But what did you think when Terry announced that Sandra would be coaching the principals?' asked Ian. 'Do you think you can cope with that?'

Sue thought for a few moments. 'Well, I'll have to. After all, she's a very experienced actress, and I need that experience. I'm less worried about Sandra than I am about Ron- I really can't imagine being romantic with him- oh dear- the idea fills me with horror!'

'You mustn't worry, Sue- you really mustn't! Old Ron's OK at heart, and once he's made-up and in costume, you'll find he's quite attractive!'

'At a distance, maybe,' replied Sue. 'I'll have to be one hell of a good actress to convince the audience- and myself- that I'm madly in love with him! Oh, for heaven's sake, Ian- pour me another glass of wine!'

Ian did as she asked, laughing at her despair.

'When are you coming round to have a go at those duets?' Sue asked. 'I just love the ones in Act II- the whole scene is beautiful, I think. It will be really useful to work on it and be word perfect before production rehearsals begin with Sandra.'

'How are you fixed on Sunday? I'm busy during the day, but I could come round about sevenish. Will your mother be free to play for us then?'

'Yes, she should be. She's on duty until about six- I'll get us all some supper, and she can relax over a nice gin and tonic, then she'll be ready to play the piano till we're exhausted. She's got more energy than I have, and once she's on that piano, it's hard to stop her!'

'Good,' said Ian. 'We'd better be on our way- I think they're wanting to close. I'll get this-' as Sue got out her purse, 'You can pay next time!'

'I certainly shall,' said Sue. 'Fair's fair- and I'd love to come here again. Maybe we can ask a couple of others to join us another time. I'd like to get to know some of them a bit better- there never seems time to chat on rehearsal nights, and once you get into the pub it's so noisy.'

'Good idea,' said Ian, as they strolled along to where Sue had left her car. 'Next time we finish early, we'll see what we can do. How about Ron, for instance? Now, *he'd* love to come- he could talk about all his former triumphs!'

Sue made a suitable grimace at Ian as she got into her car.

'See you Sunday,' she said. 'Thanks for the meal- 'bye till then.' And blowing Ian a kiss, she drove away.

Ian watched her go, a thoughtful expression on his face. He liked Sue a lot, she was fun to be with, and had a great sense of humour. However, he decided, that was all. There was no way he could contemplate a serious relationship- not in the foreseeable future. He was still missing Liz so very much, and deeply hurt by the way their relationship had ended. Nearly two and a half years ago Ian had bought a flat, and his girl friend Liz, whom he had met six months previously at a colleague's wedding, had moved in with him. As far as Ian was concerned, it was to be on a permanent basis, possibly leading to marriage. They redecorated the flat, spent hours choosing furnishings, and loved and laughed together in the attractive home they had created, completely happy in each other's company- or so Ian had thought. Liz was tall and slim, with long dark hair and brown eyes which grew bright with enthusiasm as the two of them sat drinking wine in their sunny kitchen, discussing their future together.

Then with scarcely any warning, the dream was over. Ian got home from rehearsal one night to find the flat empty, all Liz's things gone, and a letter on one of the kitchen units, propped up against the toaster. Moments passed before Ian could bring himself to open it. Her bold sprawling writing blurred before his eyes, and at first he could not read it. Now, he remembered every word on that one brief page, and always would.

'Darling Ian,' it said, 'I've loved being here with you, and in the beginning I really did think it would work. I wanted it to. But you must have noticed that for some time we've not been quite on the same wavelength- you have your operatic society (which is really not my scene!) and I have my own interests. That's not all. I've met someone else, and I've fallen completely for him, and he for me. So what can I do except say thank you for a couple of really lovely years which I shall always remember. I'm sorry to cause you sadness, but I think that you will very soon realise that I've done the right thing. Incidentally, I shall be living far away from Marleigh, so there will be no risk of our meeting. Thank you for everything. .. and I'm so sorry. Liz.'

Ian sighed, and retraced his steps to where he had parked his car. Had he and Liz gradually drifted apart? He couldn't remember their doing so. Or maybe he'd been too engrossed in the show he was involved in at the time- it had been two days before the first night when he had returned much later than usual from rehearsal and found the letter. It was now more than six months since Liz had left, and although he was outwardly his old cheerful self, the heartache remained. Should he have given up the operatic society? But he enjoyed it- he'd been a choirboy when he was young, and he still loved to sing. Then he'd met Mike Mitchell at a party, and been talked into it.

'We desperately need handsome young fellas,' Mike had joked. So Ian had gone along and become a regular member. It had never occurred to him that Liz had minded. But in any case, if she'd met someone else . . . Although so many things in the flat reminded him of her, he hadn't had the urge to move. Perhaps he still thought that she might return. . .

'No,' decided Ian firmly. ' That part of my life is most definitely over.' And after all- life wasn't so bad. . . .

Ian strode down the street whistling a tune from 'The Pirates of Penzance' till he reached his car.

Two days later Sheila Allen and Mike Mitchell sat at a small table in a village pub ten miles from Marleigh, confident that no-one who knew them would be likely to be there. A log fire burned brightly in the hearth, and the heavily-beamed interior was cosy and comforting. Mike was his usual relaxed self, but Sheila was tense- he could sense that. He took her hand in his- it was trembling slightly, and his grip tightened.

'Stop it, Sheila,' he said. 'You're here with me, we're miles away from Marleigh. We have to talk things over- see what to do- when, where and how.' A sudden, awful thought struck him. 'You haven't changed your mind, have you, Sheila?'

'Oh, Mike, no . . . . it's just that- I don't know how to tell Brian . . . as for the kids-'

'Look, my darling- there's only one thing which stands in the way at present- something we can't get out of- and that's the show. That has to be got over before we tell anyone anything. It's April now, we rehearse till July. Then we have August off, back in September for intensive rehearsals till the end of October, then the show. Till then, we have to go on as usual- you, as far as the family is concerned, and I with Jackie. There is absolutely no point in going through what will obviously be a traumatic experience for everyone concerned before 'Pirates'. The old adage 'the show must go on' is absolutely right.'

'But how can we concentrate on our roles, work as normal, with such drama and disruption ahead?' Sheila's brow was furrowed with anxiety.

'Many actors have given their best performances under terrible stress,' said Mike. 'As soon as you get on stage, something happens. You switch off your private life, take on the life of your character- that's how it works, Sheila, I promise you.'

'Then the last night arrives- the party- the family come round backstage. . what an act we shall have to put on, Mike! All joy and excitement- than next day the bombshell-'

'I want you as soon as we can manage it,' said Mike. 'Oh, how I want you! But it doesn't have to be the very next day- we'll have the rest of our lives together, after all, my darling. Let the excitement of the show die down, talk to Brian quietly some time during the following week- choose your moment-'

'There will never be a moment,' said Sheila sadly. 'How *can* there be? This will be the most terrible thing I have ever done- hurting three innocent people so much- spoiling their lives- oh, Mike- I have so much more to give up than you-'

Mike looked hurt, and Sheila was immediately contrite.

'I meant- I have three people's lives to upset- you have only one- and you say your relationship is over anyway. It will surely be less hard for you.'

'I see what you mean, but it will still be a shock for Jackie- after all, we've been married so long. She will be hurt when I tell her it's over. It won't be easy. But I do understand what it will be like for you.'

'Tell me, Mike- if I leave Brian-'

'*If?* Mike was angry. 'What d'you mean- *if?*'

'I mean *when*- of course I do! When I leave Brian, where do we go? What shall we do?' Sheila looked at Mike, her eyes anxious.

'To start with, I'm going to have to get a job transfer,' said Mike. 'And I happen to know there's going to be a vacancy in our Oxford branch in the autumn- I can put in for that at the right time.'

Mike worked in financial services, a job he loved and was very good at. 'And there's a splendid operatic society there, darling- what d'you think about that? They put on their shows at a big theatre, too- now, that would be a step up, wouldn't it?'

Sheila tried to smile, but her thoughts were on her family and the upheaval she was going to inflict on them. Joining another operatic society was the last thing on her mind just then.

'You don't think Brian would stop me from seeing Matt and Emma, do you? I couldn't bear that-'

'Of course he wouldn't,' said Mike soothingly. 'Brian's a nice guy- when he's got used to the situation I'm sure he'll do his best to see that things go smoothly. He won't make difficulties, he's not that sort.'

'Where shall we live? We can't stay in Marleigh, that would be impossible,' said Sheila.

Mike got to his feet. Maybe another drink would help Sheila relax, and see things his way.

'I'm getting you a G&T,' he said. 'And a double, at that.'

Sheila watched him as he went to get the drinks, leaning casually on the counter and chatting with easy charm to the girl behind the bar, who smiled back at him. What an attractive man he was- could he really want to spend the rest of his like with *her*? What did he see in her, a housewife and mother- ordinary, dull, plain. . . But in this, she was completely wrong.

Sheila may not have been a beauty, but plain she was not. She had an attractively rounded figure, and her face, though in many ways unremarkable, was redeemed by expressive, almost green eyes and a generous mouth. But her best feature was her glorious auburn hair. No, Sheila was not plain, and no-one knew that better than Mike. He wanted Sheila, and he was going to have her. He set the drinks down on the table, pouring the tonic into Sheila's glass, stopping when she indicated.

'Now, drink that, my darling,' said Mike. 'And you'll soon feel much better about everything.'

'I hope I'll soon be able to do that without having to resort to drink,' said Sheila with a faint laugh, but after taking a few sips, she did begin to relax. Things would work out. They must.

'Now, you asked where we should live. I've had an idea. The chap who's leaving the job I have my eye on is moving south- he's getting married. He's got a flat in Oxford- it may be small, as he's been there on his own, but I'm going to see if I can take it over when he goes. That would be a very good stepping stone for us. We needn't stay there long, but it would give us some breathing space until we can see where we'd like to live.'

'That sounds a good idea,' said Sheila, trying to imagine living in a small flat with Mike after the large untidy house she shared with Brian, noisy with the music and shouting of two lively teenagers.

Mike moved closer to her and slid his arm round her, his fingers sensuous and demanding. Sheila was amazed at the response she felt at his touch. Nothing else seemed to matter. She wanted this man so intensely that everything else- Brian, Matt, Emma- seemed to pale into insignificance. Part of her was shocked that she could feel like that, but desire for Mike overwhelmed her, and she could not resist it.

'Come on, my darling, it's only quarter to nine. You won't be expected back till ten or so, will you? I know a place we can drive to where we'll be alone- just the two of us.' They finished their drinks in silence, then left the pub, walking slowly back to Mike's car. His arm tightened around her. He pulled her roughly towards him and kissed her, and she knew that she was lost.

CHAPTER 13

There was a lot of activity amongst the committee members of Marleigh Operatic Society the day before production rehearsals began on 'The Pirates of Penzance.'

Eileen hurried through the market square with a purposeful air and into the cosy warmth of the Copper Kettle Tea Rooms. Norma was already seated at a corner table, and Eileen sank into a vacant chair with a sigh of relief.

'I'm not late, am I, Norma?' she said. 'I couldn't get a space in the car park for ages- went round and round- it's very busy for a Monday, isn't it?'

'I noticed there was more traffic than usual,' said Norma. 'But you're not late at all, I've only just arrived myself. Two coffees, please- oh, make it a pot for two,' she said to the hovering waitress.

'What news?' asked Eileen. 'Doreen's contacted some costume hire firms, I believe?'

'Oh, yes,' replied Norma, getting a notebook from her handbag. 'Three, actually, but there's one which seems much better than the other two, in price and availability. What's more, they seem quite interested in what we're going to do, and came up with some useful suggestions. I had a long telephone conversation with such a nice woman. We can go and see the costumes and pick out what we want any Wednesday between the hours of ten and four.'

'Sounds promising, said Eileen, consulting her diary. 'How about going Wednesday week? If you can make the rehearsal tomorrow, we could take the girls' measurements. If there are any absentees we'd have the following Tuesday as well.'

'That's a good idea. George can come with me tomorrow and measure the men.' Norma made a note in her book.

'Excellent. Then we can go and see what costumes are on offer. I know it seems early- goodness, it's only May, and our show isn't till October-'

'I know, but don't you remember- one year we left it rather late, and the best ones had gone. We had very little choice,' said Norma.

'That's true. By the way, where is this firm?' asked Eileen.

'Birmingham. And I understand it's not far from New Street Station, so we can go by train and have a nice day out. I'll treat you to lunch.' Norma put away her notebook. 'This coffee's getting cold. D'you think we could run to another pot?'

'Of course,' said Eileen. 'And how about one of those Danish pastries- they look delicious.'

'All right,' laughed Norma. 'After all, no-one's going to take *our* measurements !'

Sandra looked at the clock on her bedside table. It was the little gold alarm clock Fred had given her as a good luck present on one of her first nights. Eight-fifteen a.m. and she was due at Terry's salon at eight-thirty. The appointment was an early one, but he had obligingly fitted her in at short notice. Sandra had caught sight of herself in the mirror the day before and been shocked. She decided that something must be done to help regain her customary well-groomed appearance before she met some of the principal members of the cast to begin her coaching rehearsals. After all, she had not seen many of them since the auditions, and no-one must have any idea of what she had been through, or suspect that her relationship with Fred was at breaking point. If only he would talk. . . . . But Sandra dare not broach the painful subject which had brought about their estrangement, she simply could not. Yet until they had talked about it and she had the opportunity to pour out her heart to him and convince him of the remorse she felt, it would stand solidly between them- an impenetrable barrier to their reconciliation.

Sandra went to the bedroom door and listened. The front door closed quietly. Fred had gone to work- now she was free to go downstairs without fear of meeting him. How different from the way it used to be- he would have brought her a cup of tea in bed, and they would have had breakfast together, chatting about things in general, and society matters in particular. She would always stand at the front door and wave until his car turned the corner. Tears came to her eyes, but she refused to give way. Picking up her car keys from the hall table, Sandra put on her coat and left the house.

Terry welcomed her into the salon, kissed her on both cheeks and ushered her to a washbasin. Summoning a junior to shampoo her hair, he smiled reassuringly.

'We'll soon have you looking a million dollars,' he said. 'I'm not in a rush this morning- Mondays are always quiet- so we can chat as I work.'

Soon Sandra was sitting in front of the mirror, watching Terry as he skilfully re-shaped her neglected hair.

'My, you *have* let it go,' he said reprovingly. 'But we'll soon have it back to normal.'

'I know,' sighed Sandra, 'But I haven't had the heart to do anything. Even just looking after the house has taken all my energy, and-' She broke off, unable to talk about her estrangement from Fred.

But Terry understood. Eileen had partly put him in the picture, without betraying Sandra's confidence completely. 'Things no better?' he asked.

Sandra shook her head. 'No. We just live in the same house. That's all.'

'Give it time,' Terry said soothingly. 'Don't rush things.' He decided it was better not to dwell on Sandra's unhappiness. 'Now, remind me- who are you rehearsing with tomorrow?

'Well, you've made me jump in at the deep end,' said Sandra with a wry smile. Your schedule states that I begin with Mabel and Frederic's scenes in Act II. That's a hurdle I hadn't expected to negotiate till a bit later on.'

'I did that on purpose,' replied Terry. 'Much better that you should start right away with the two 'lovers'- after all, you know exactly what is wanted there. I knew you'd be dreading it, so why not confront it straight away? It'll be down hill all the way after that.'

'I suppose so. What d'you think Sue will be like to work with? Will she take direction from me?'

'I should think so!' said Terry emphatically. 'Sue knows nothing of stagecraft, though I wouldn't be surprised if you find she's a natural. And she's a very nice lass- I'm sure she realises how lucky she is to be able to work with you. There!' Sandra was ready to go under the drier. 'I think you'll be delighted when I've combed you out. Debbie!' he called, 'Put Mrs Ogilvie under the drier, please- and bring her a cup of coffee. See you in about twenty minutes,' he said to Sandra, with a comforting pat on the shoulder. 'Now, you just relax with your coffee and a nice magazine,' And Terry scurried away to his next client.

Sandra did as she was told. Perhaps everything would turn out all right in the end. She would just have to be patient and take each day as it came.

'Mum! Where are my new trainers? I can't find them anywhere!' Matt's anguished voice floated down the stairs.

Sheila put another couple of slices of bread in the toaster.

'In the hall, where you left them,' she called. 'And hurry up! It's nearly quarter past eight- you'll be late, both of you.'

 Emma burst into the kitchen. 'I've lost my maths prep,' she moaned. 'I put it somewhere safe, and I've forgotten where!'

'What's that on top of the fridge?' asked Sheila. 'Is that it?'

Emma seized upon the dog-eared exercise book with relief.

'Thanks, Mum,' she said, 'You're great- you always know where things are! Old Cleggie goes mad if we don't hand in our books first thing Monday morning- you know what she's like- no, I don't want any breakfast-'

'You're not going to school without something,' insisted Sheila. 'Here- have a bowl of cereal at least- then I'll let you off.'

Emma sat down at the table with a sigh of resignation. She knew how far she could go. Matt appeared on the scene next, trainers in hand, and flopped into a chair. He gulped his glass of orange juice rapidly, and reached out for a piece of toast, putting on his trainers as he ate it noisily.

'Come on, Em,' he said, his mouth full, 'Time we left.' The pair of them jumped up and made a dash for the door.

'Lunch boxes!' reminded Sheila, 'By the freezer- oh, what are you two like?'

'Thanks, Mum!' said Emma, giving her mother a lightning hug.

'See you later!' added Matt, as they dashed out of the front door and down the path.

Sheila sank exhausted into a chair and reached automatically for the teapot. Pouring herself a cup of the rather stewed brew, she gave a long sigh. What would the children do when she was no longer there to make sure they had some breakfast, didn't forget their lunch, and to help them to find things? How would they manage? Brian left the house at ten to eight, so he would not be around to see them off to school. Then, suddenly, she thought of Mike, and her tensed-up body relaxed. The mundane routine of getting Matt and Emma to school in time, making up their lunch boxes, seeing that they had everything they needed, paled into insignificance. She had a life, too, and it was out there, waiting for her. At the moment she was there to do everything for them, but surely, at fifteen and seventeen they should be standing on their own feet, doing more for themselves, learning to be independent. She would try to start that process now, encouraging them to remember where they put things, perhaps even get them ready the night before- yes, that would help. If she could persuade them into some sort of routine now, that would solve a lot of problems in advance. Getting to school, thank goodness, would be the least of their worries. Marleigh Comprehensive was less than ten minutes' walk from the house. Matt and Emma usually set off together, but by the time they reached the end of the road, each had met up with a crowd of friends. They'd soon get used to the new way, thought Sheila, I've been spoiling them- waiting on them hand and foot. Brian, too.

At that moment the phone rang. Mike's voice was warm and comforting, and at the sound of it, any doubts that Sheila had been trying to suppress vanished immediately.

'All right, darling?' he said. 'I know it's a good time to call you, and I realise you sometimes need a little reassurance- especially on a dreary Monday morning. Nothing to say- except- I love you.' And the line went dead.

Sheila put down the receiver and stood looking at it for a few seconds. Then she smiled. What had she been worrying about?

George and Desmond sat over a couple of pints in the snug at the Coach and Horses. They had been discussing football most of the evening, but now their attention turned to matters operatic.

'How's the design for the programme coming on?' asked Desmond.

'Rather well,' replied George. 'You know old Charlie Hanson- he's one of the policemen? He's the art teacher at Marleigh Grammar, and a bit of an artist in his own right -'

'Yes, I know Charlie,' laughed Desmond, 'he's the one who starts on his left foot when all the others start on the right!'

'That's him! And marches upstage when everyone else marches down!'

Both men had a chuckle at memories of Charlie's stage exploits, then George became serious.

'He may not know what he's doing on stage, but he knows what to do where draftsmanship is concerned. He's given me some marvellous sketches for the front of the programme- witty, humorous, and very nineteen-twenties. Damn! I meant to bring them with me tonight. Never mind, I'll let you see them tomorrow. We'll need to have a meeting to decide which design to choose- that'll be quite a job- they're all so good.' George finished off his pint. 'Another?' he asked.

'Oh, just a half,' said Desmond. 'That's bloody good news about the programme. We'll need to keep the twenties idea to ourselves till the last minute, so we'd better be careful about the posters, but it'll be fine to have it on the front of the programmes.'

'Just what I thought,' agreed George, going to fetch the drinks.

Returning a few minutes later, he set the glasses down on the table, and resumed his seat.

'Well, Desmond- first production rehearsal tomorrow,' he said. 'Will you be there? I'll have the designs with me.'

'Cheers,' said Desmond, slurping his beer noisily. 'Oh yes, I'll look in. Terry's blocking the opening- you know, the Pirates' chorus, with the Pirate King and Ruth. I'll have a look at that.'

'And it'll be Sandra's first rehearsal with Sue. I see from the schedule that she's setting the second act scene with Mabel and Frederic. She'll feel rather strange, I should imagine. How d'you think she'll cope?' George looked thoughtful.

'Oh, Sandra will be OK. She's too much of a pro. to let her feelings show. And Sue will be very co-operative, I'm sure. Ron's more likely to be a problem than her, I bet,' said Desmond.

'Ron? Why should he be a problem? He knows the part backwards.'

'That's the trouble,' replied Desmond. 'He's a bit inflexible. If Sandra has any new ideas, he's sure to say, 'but we didn't do that in nineteen seventy-eight' and embarrass her terribly!'

'Oh, surely not,' said George. 'He's not going to want to draw attention to his age when he's trying to act twenty-one!'

'We'll see,' said Desmond. 'But one thing we do know- it's going to be a production with a difference!'

Mike leaned back in his comfortable armchair, enjoying a large scotch and soda. He stretched luxuriously, his mind filled with thoughts of Sheila, the show, and how the future might work out. He wouldn't see her tomorrow as she was called for rehearsal of the Act I opening scenes, in which he was not involved, but they'd arrange to meet somehow- later in the week. Mike found the excitement and risk associated with their clandestine rendez-vous intensely stimulating. He had not considered how he might find life with Sheila when these aspects had been removed, and their relationship established on a permanent basis. All he knew was that she was for the moment unattainable, and therefore he wanted her, and intended to have her. He enjoyed the delight and fulfilment Sheila so obviously experienced when he made love to her, and her ready response to the new and overwhelming sensations she discovered under his expert tuition. She would go wherever he led her, and this thought was exhilarating to him.

Mike picked up his glass from the small table beside him and sipped his scotch slowly, his thoughts on the next encounter he would have with Sheila . . . soon, he hoped.

The door to the living room opened and Jackie came in.

'Pour me a gin, darling- not too much tonic, but plenty of ice-well, you know how I like it.'

 Mike rose to do as she asked, and Jackie lay back on the sofa with a sigh. He brought up a small table and put her gin and tonic where she could reach it.

'Thanks- you're a star,' said Jackie, taking a long drink. 'Just what the doctor ordered.'

Mike returned to his comfortable chair and regarded his wife critically. She had just come out of the shower, and was wearing a white towelling robe which parted to show her long slim legs, still tanned from a recent business trip with her boss to Antigua. Her dark hair, damp from the shower, was piled up on top of her head, some tendrils escaping in little curls round her face. which was still flushed from the heat. Mike considered his wife thoughtfully. Jackie was undoubtedly a very attractive woman- it was hard to believe she was getting on for forty. Where had they gone wrong? They were still fond of each other, of course, but how long had it been since he had made love to her? Mike had lost count. But as he watched Jackie sipping her drink, he was struck by an overwhelming urge to touch her- possess her. . . He struggled to resist it, but tonight there seemed to be an unusual

glow about her- a strangeness that he found intensely disturbing.
. . exciting, even. . . Mike felt his desire mounting. . . He put his
glass down slowly, and looked across at his wife.

His eyes met hers, and she smiled. 'Shall we have another?' she
asked.

Mike did not reply. Crossing to where she lay, he put out his
hands and pulled her to her feet.

'Not tonight,' he said slowly. 'I think it's time for bed.'

CHAPTER 14

'Gather round, chaps,' said Terry, clapping his hands for attention, 'and let's see what we're going to do.' Clad in his rehearsal outfit of white jeans and mauve sweatshirt, he appeared on the surface to be a rather effete figure, which was not the case at all. When Terry called for attention there was an immediate hush. He was able to exert discipline when required, and exercised a quiet authority that commanded respect.

There were plenty of laughs during rehearsals, and Terry was the first to appreciate a joke, but he worked the cast quite hard, and they admired him for it, as the results were almost always rewarding.

'Now, most of you know what this opera's all about,' said Terry, 'but there are one or two new ones among you, so let's explain the opening section, which we're going to block tonight. As the curtain goes up, all the pirates are celebrating Fred's birthday-he's twenty-one- at least, he thinks he is-'

At that moment some wag at the back called out, 'Good old Ron!'

Terry chose to ignore the interruption, which was greeted with a few sniggers, quickly suppressed.

'It isn't until Act II he learns that as he was born in leap year on February 29th, he's actually still legally only five and a quarter! But that doesn't concern us yet- we're concentrating on the birthday celebrations, and I've had a really novel idea for the opening. The cue for the curtain to rise is on the fifteenth bar of the introduction, but we're changing all that! The house tabs will go out as soon as the music starts. I've managed to locate an old horn gramophone, and we're going to have the first part of the intro played on that, the orchestra quietly taking over on the fifteenth bar, when the curtain usually rises.' There were murmurs of approval at this, and Terry continued: 'That's the perfect place for the orchestra to come in- I think it'll be marvellous- and it will establish the period we're setting the opera in, right at the beginning.'

Sounds good,' remarked Ian to Sheila, 'trust Terry to come up with a bit of theatrical magic!'

'Well, I hope the gramophone will play it in the same key as the band,' laughed Sheila. 'You know what those old recordings are like.'

'All part of the fun,' Ian said. 'Anything for a laugh!'

'Now, let's not waste any time,' said Terry, in a business-like way. 'Will someone put a chair centre right- thank you, Charlie- a bit further upstage please- yes, that's it. That's a rock, boys, by the way.. And we need another rock stage left- that stool there will do, Ian- thanks. Now, the gramophone will pre-set be on the right hand rock- Ian, you'll be winding it when the curtain rises, so would you go and stand there, please.' Ian did as requested, and Terry surveyed the rest of his pirate band.

'Now, we need a small group around the gramophone- you three go and join Ian- one of you sitting on the ground, stage right, one behind, and you, Hamish, slightly behind Ian. Don't hide yourself- there's plenty of room, and Ian's got a solo to sing in a minute, so he'll be moving away.'

In no time at all Terry had arranged the men in interesting groups, dressing the stage effectively.

'Ian, you'll have one of the sherry flasks, and pour some out for the men nearest you between the verses of your solo. Ben-' Terry addressed another pirate, 'You have the other flask, and do the same the other side. OK?' Ben nodded. Terry looked round for Sheila.

'Ah, there you are, Ruth. I want you to make your entrance when the men begin the last chorus, carrying a birthday cake for Frederic. Come down centre, hold it out to him, and he must blow out the candle- we'll just have the one- and we'll have to consult the fire regulations about that- on the very last note. That'll take a bit of timing- where is Ron, by the way?'

'He was in the pub just now,' volunteered one of the basses.

Terry grimaced, and was just about to send someone to fetch him, when he appeared, singing, 'Pour, oh pour the pirate sherry,' the words of the opening chorus, in an a raucous tenor.

'Thank you, Ron- we'll let you know,' said Terry, to the amusement of the pirates, 'Go and sit stage left, please. No need to tell you how to react in this scene- you know what it's all about. Now, let's sing through the opening, and see how we get on. By the way, you'll be presented with a birthday cake, Ron, during the last chorus- think you can blow out the candle on the last note?'

'No problem,' said Ron. 'Now, where's that pirate sherry?'

The men laughed as Ron took his place, and Terry went over to Sarah Blyth, the accompanist, who was ready at the piano.

'OK, Sarah- let's see what they can do- we'll go right through the opening without stopping, regardless of mistakes. Stand by, everyone.'

The first attempt was not too bad, but Terry was far from satisfied.

'Really, chaps! You're *pirates*- act like it! Rough and ready, and a lot more animation. I know you're all 'noblemen who have gone wrong'- but you went wrong quite a long time ago, don't forget! You're more piratical than noble by now- and this is a celebration- let your hair down- you've been imbibing sherry, and you're all pretty rowdy. Let's have a bit of acting- thank you, Sarah!'

The second attempt at the opening scene was much more successful after Terry's lecture. Halfway through it, the door opened and Sandra appeared, Sue close behind her. They stood and watched, and Sue applauded at the end of the scene. Terry turned round to see who it was, and went to kiss Sandra.

'Hello, both of you. Goodness, is it eight o'clock already? Ron- you're going with Sandra and Sue now, to rehearse in the other room, aren't you? Ah, here's your accompanist- hello, Tom. Aren't we lucky to have two marvellous pianists? Off you go, then- we'll be having a coffee break in-' Terry consulted his watch, 'about three quarters of an hour- see you then. Now, boys- once again, please. Come on slightly earlier with that cake,

Sheila, and show it around a bit more to the pirates, otherwise it won't register with the audience. Then we'll go on, so stand by, Chris, for the dialogue leading into the your song.'

Terry worked on tirelessly, choreographing the Pirate King's song in a splendid, swashbuckling way. Chris Hatton was the perfect choice for the part- tall, broad, with a ringing bass-baritone voice and a good presence. He was quick to follow Terry's direction, and inspired the pirates to react in a much more lusty way. Terry was extremely pleased with the way things were shaping. He wondered how Sandra was coping in the other room.

Sandra had taken great care with her appearance that evening. Her hair looked lovely; Terry had achieved exactly the right effect, beautifully styled, but soft and natural. She was wearing a navy trouser suit of a casual cut, with a cream silk shirt, and she had taken a long time putting on her make-up; the result was very attractive, and helped to give her some of the confidence she needed so much. She had gone downstairs to find Fred was still there, sitting in his favourite chair and reading the paper.

'I'm going out, Fred,' she said tentatively. 'Terry's asked me to help with the production, and coach some of the principals.'

'Oh,' was Fred's monosyllabic reply.

'I shan't be late. Goodbye,' she said, and left quietly, closing the door behind her.

When she had gone, Fred put his paper down. The expression on his face was one of extreme sadness, and he gave a deep sigh.

As Sandra drove to the hall, her feelings were very mixed. Had she done the right thing in agreeing to take these rehearsals? Could she really face it? It was too late to withdraw now, and she'd have to go through with it. She couldn't let Terry down. As she got out of her car she came face to face with Sue. Sue felt just as awkward as Sandra, but swiftly decided that the best thing to do was to take the bull by the horns.

'Hello, Sandra,' she said brightly. 'I'm really glad you're going to be coaching us. I've got so much to learn- I haven't done much acting, you know-'

Sandra smiled. Perhaps this wasn't going to be so bad. 'We've all got to start somewhere,' she said. 'I'm sure we'll get on just fine.'

As they entered the hall and watched the men rehearsing, Sandra took a deep breath. This was the world she knew, these were her friends. The greetings she received from everyone, the smiles, the waves- all this made her feel better than she had done for weeks- in fact, she felt suddenly confident.

'Come on, Ron,' she said, 'let's get this scene sorted out- I'm going to give it a new look!'

Ron looked surprised, but followed Sandra and Sue meekly out of the hall. Once in the smaller rehearsal room, Sandra took command.

'Nice to see you again, Tom,' she said to the accompanist, who was already seated at the piano. 'It seem ages, doesn't it?'

Tom was a plain young man with glasses, who played the piano brilliantly. He looked at Sandra admiringly.

'Hello, Sandra- my, you do look well. I'm looking forward to this.'

'So am I,' she replied, surprised to find that she actually was. 'Let's just sing through this scene first, to get in the mood before we start to block it. I'll just sit and listen. Thank you, Tom.'

Sandra sat back and gave her full attention to the singing, with mixed feelings. But what a lovely voice Sue had- so young and fresh. There was no doubt that she would make a delightful Mabel. And seeing Ron, middle-aged, and looking it, made Sandra realise that it was right that she herself should not be playing an ingenue any longer. Nor should Ron, of course, but it seemed at the moment that there was no-one to follow in his footsteps. His voice was showing signs of wear, and was too loud and forceful throughout. She resolved to try and deal with that, though it would not be easy.

Step by step Sandra worked through the scene, placing Sue in strategically advantageous positions to counteract Ron's over-blown performance. She tried to tone down the volume of his singing, and occasionally succeeded in doing so, much to her surprise. When they came to that most poignant of duets, 'Ah, leave me not to pine alone and desolate', Sandra knew she must arrange it so that Sue was able to project her voice, and Ron was in a less good position to do so. The duet is often performed with Frederic seated, and Mabel kneeling at his feet, but Sandra, much to Ron's dismay, decided to stage it the other way round. This seemed to do the trick, and the voices balanced more evenly. Sandra was as tactful as possible with Ron, realising that it was the best way to deal with him.

'You can sing much more softly here, Ron,' she said more than once. 'Your voice comes over so well, you don't need to push it-in fact, your quiet singing is most effective.'

'Oh,' said Ron, taken off his guard, 'Do you think so? Oh well, I'll try it that way, then.'

Sandra was quick to encourage Sue, who at the beginning of rehearsal had been somewhat diffident. Terry had been right- she was a natural, and picked up the moves, and the emotions and gestures which went with them very quickly. The coffee break seemed to come in no time, and they all went into the main hall for this, except Ron, who vanished out of the door, presumably to the pub.

Ian sought out Sue, to find out how things were going in the other room.

'Really well,' she said. 'Sandra's so good- I'm learning fast. But Ron- ugh! He's so coarse, and smells of whisky- it's revolting. If I manage to make those love scenes convincing, I'll be nominated for an Oscar!'

Ian laughed heartily. 'Oh, you'll be fine. He'll be much better in performance, you'll see.'

'What about *you*?' asked Sue. 'How's the opening coming on? The bit I saw looked very promising, I thought.'

'Oh, it's fine. But we need the props for the full effect.' And Ian described the business with the old gramophone.

'Wonderful! Oh, it sounds really good-'

'It will be, I think. Terry's full of ideas- he's not just a pretty face,' laughed Ian.'Let's see if we can grab another coffee before we start again. Being a pirate's thirsty work-so's being a prima donna, I suppose!' he teased.

Sue made a most unladylike sign at Ian, and they both laughed.

Terry was chatting to Sandra; he had managed to get her on her own to see how she was coping. He was pleasantly surprised to find that she was actually enjoying what she was doing, enthusiastic about Sue's potential, and the way she was taking on board Sandra's suggestions.

'And Ron?' asked Terry. 'Any problems there?'

'Nothing intentional,' replied Sandra. 'But I have to say they don't make a very credible pair of lovers. Sue's so young compared with Ron- there's nothing we can do about that, of course- it's something we have to live with. But oh, Terry- it's made me see how right it is for me not to play Mabel even if I could sing it!' she added with a wry smile. 'Seeing Ron trying to play a twenty-one year old- I've learned my lesson well and truly.'

'Oh, Sandra,' laughed Terry, 'It's so good to see you enjoying yourself- and I really believe you are. But remember- you haven't given up the bright lights for ever. There's sure to be a show sooner or later with a part tailor-made for you- meanwhile, I suspect you're having quite a good time, aren't you?'

'Yes,' said Sandra, surprised at herself, 'I really believe I am! And you know, Terry, I'm managing to restrain Ron's singing a bit- paying him compliments when he sings softly- whether he'll keep it up when he gets on stage, goodness knows- he may go back to his permanent fortissimo then, knowing we can do nothing about it!'

'You're doing well, Sandra,' said Terry. 'I knew you'd enjoy coaching once you started. And I was sure you'd be good at it.'

'Terry!' George called across the hall. 'Oh, and Sandra, too- can you spare a minute?'

Terry looked at the clock. 'Just one, George- then we must get back to work. The girls are arriving- I promised them half an hour on the Charleston when the boys are finished. And I know Norma wants to take some measurements. Come on, Sandra-George has some programme designs, if I'm not mistaken.'

They went over to where George and Norma were standing. Charlie Hanson was hovering nearby.

'Have a look at these,' said George. 'What do you think of them?'

The drawings were delightful, and it was hard to believe they had been the work of the rather ungainly baritone reputed to have two left feet. One depicted a nineteen-twenties flapper in mid-Charleston, a pirate and a policeman peering round a rock on each side. The others were equally imaginative, and all were executed with wit and skill.

'Just look at that!' Terry squealed with delight. 'Oh my, just what we want, Charlie, you *are* a clever one.'

'They'll have to go before the committee-' said George, 'and you've given us quite a problem, Charlie-'

Charlie looked worried.

'They're all so good- it'll be terribly difficult choosing which one to use. We'll have to take a vote on it. Thanks a lot, they're excellent.'

Charlie beamed. He would not worry about his feet so much now.

'Here's Eileen,' said Norma. 'And quite a few of the girls are here. We can start taking measurements, then you can do the men when Terry's finished with them, George.'

The men resumed their stage positions, and Sandra and her group made their way to the other room. Ron appeared from his refreshment in the Marleigh Arms in the nick of time, and work began again. Sandra finished the scene, then began at the beginning again, stopping and starting in order to criticise, change where necessary and put in detail.

'Don't grab Sue quite so energetically, Ron,' she said. 'I know we've updated the show, but remember, it's still only the nine-teen-twenties, and people were more restrained than we are today- that's better,' as Ron relaxed his grip. 'There's one thing we haven't dealt with yet- and that's the date. Originally Frederic says, referring to his real twenty-first- 'That birthday will not be reached by me till nineteen-forty.' Well, as we're already in the twenties that doesn't make sense, so we've decided to change it to the 'nineteen-eighties'. It's not possible to be more exact, because the words wouldn't scan. Is that OK? Let's try it.'

Once more through, and it was time to stop. Sandra suddenly felt quite exhausted- she hadn't realised how hard she had been concentrating.

'I don't know when we'll have another chance to go through this scene,' she said. 'But do try and remember what we've accomplished tonight. I know you've done it several times before, Ron, but we've put in some very different moves, and the fact that it has been updated means that we have to see it through slightly different eyes.'

Ron, already halfway through the door on his way to the Marleigh Arms, blew Sandra a kiss, and assured her he'd give it some thought.

"Bye, Sandra, 'bye, Sue, 'bye, Tom,' he called, and disappeared.

Tom, putting his music away, smiled at Sandra. 'I thought that was an excellent rehearsal,' he said. 'You gave that scene a whole new approach- it seemed so fresh to me, though I've played it a hundred times.'

'I'm glad,' said Sandra. 'That's really good to hear- I feel that what I've been trying to achieve has worked.' She turned to Sue. 'And knowing your words and music so well helped no end, Sue. It meant we could get on straight away on the production.'

'Well, it's compliments all round, then,' answered Sue. 'Because I've learned a lot tonight, thanks to you, Sandra.'

Sandra declined an invitation from Terry to go for a drink after rehearsal. She felt that she was not yet quite ready for the laughter and chat in the Marleigh Arms- people would ask where Fred was, and she couldn't bear that. He often used to come with her to rehearsal, or for a drink afterwards.

Maybe I'll go next time, she thought- I've got to stand on my own feet. I've got past the worst bit, now.

Sandra got into her car, fastened her seat belt, and sat for a few moments without moving. It seemed rather an anti-climax just to drive straight home. She thought of the many evenings she'd gone to the pub with everyone, exchanging gossip, laughing and chatting until they were all turned out. Maybe she'd soon be doing that again. But would Fred be there?

CHAPTER 15

'Bit further upstage, Ian!'

'OK, Desmond- how's that?'

'Just about right- now the other one-' Ian was helping Desmond to set the stage for Act I of Pirates, marking the entrances on the floor with masking tape, and placing various substitute pieces of scenery in their correct positions. The hall was buzzing with activity. George was discussing props with Martin and Laura Wilson, who regularly conjured up the most amazing items out of next to nothing, with marvellous ingenuity. Not all were ready at this stage, but they had thoughtfully provided alternatives which could be used for the time being. Norma was surrounded by a crowd of girls who were bombarding her with questions about shoes and tights, which she was trying to answer as best she could. Doreen, sheaves of paper in her arms, was giving out rehearsal schedules leading up to the week of performances.

Sandra was deep in conversation with Terry about some tricky bit of business which did not quite work, and Eileen was discussing nineteen-twenties hairstyles with Vera, Gladys and the two other older ladies. As a background to all this hubbub, several basses were checking up on one of their more difficult vocal lines with Tom, the rehearsal pianist, who was thumping out the notes on the piano.

Terry and his team had worked hard throughout June and July, and the August break was fast approaching. There would be no rehearsals during the holiday month, when everyone would have plenty of time to forget all they had learned- or so Terry declared. This happened every year, but he soon had the company in good shape again, with intensive rehearsals and a final polish during September. All would be ready, of this Terry had no doubt, by the second week in October- performance week. It was useless to try and plan any rehearsals during August, with so many people away, and children home from school. Experience had taught the committee to suspend rehearsals until September, and this seemed to work well.

Tonight was a very important landmark in the schedule; the company were assembling in the church hall for the first run-through of the show, and it was the last time they would meet till rehearsals resumed after the break. Sue was chatting to Sharon and Angie, who had just arrived. The two girls had been antagonistic at the beginning, but had gradually warmed to her when they heard her sing, and understood why she had been cast. They saw how Sandra had taken Sue under her wing, not seeming to resent the fact that the younger girl had taken her place, and also that she seemed very happy in her new position as Terry's assistant. Sue was relieved by this change of heart- nothing was worse than a hostile atmosphere. Sharon and Angie were great fun once the barriers were down, and many were the furtive giggles they all had over the antics of various members of the cast. Sue felt that she was among friends now, and this gave her added confidence. Ron was enough to deal with, without any other complications. She found the tender scenes with Frederic very hard to make convincing, but Sandra seemed pleased with her, and Sue had to be content with that. She suspected that Ron had not been entirely sober at any of the rehearsals, and hoped desperately that he would cut down on his drinking during performance week.

Mike Mitchell strolled into the hall in leisurely fashion. He was in no hurry, for he did not make his entrance till halfway through the first act. He looked around for Sheila, and spotted her sitting by the stage area, watching Ian and Desmond setting up. Mike crept up behind her and put his arms round her. Sheila, startled, turned round to see who it was.

'Mike!' she said, 'Don't do that! Someone might see-'

Mike laughed. 'And if they did? It's no more than I often do to Angie- or any of the girls- what are you worried about?'

Sheila relaxed slightly. 'It's just that- well, when you do that to me, it's different, somehow- and I don't want anyone to have any suspicions- not at this stage, anyway.'

'You win,' said Mike. 'I'll be the soul of discretion from now on. See you afterwards, eh?' And with a suggestive wink he wandered off to have a word with Chris Hatton, who was examining the sword he would use as Pirate King.

Terry and Sandra seemed to have sorted out their problem. 'That seems to be OK then darling,' he said. Sandra nodded.

'Yes. I think we've solved it,' she answered. 'We'll try it that way tonight, and see.' After the trauma she had been through during the past few months, Sandra was a different person. Now confident and self-assured, she had thrown herself wholeheartedly into her new role of production assistant, and contrary to her expectations, was enjoying it enormously. Passing on her years of experience to Sue had not been the nightmare she had anticipated, and the idea of her possible return to a singing role when a suitable opportunity arose buoyed up her hopes for the future. Life was not so bad- even her relationship with Fred was easier now, though by no means had it returned to its former loving and intimate state. The matter which had caused such distress had never been discussed since that fateful night.

Sandra knew that until it was brought out into the open and talked over so that she could help Fred to understand and try to forgive her, they would not be able to move on. Her shameful confession would always stand between them. If she had not been so involved with the show it would have been hard for her to cope, but the complete absorption in her work had been invaluable.

Terry finished his conversation with Sandra, and looked at his watch. 'Time we got started,' he said. 'Desmond- are we ready?'

'OK, I think,' replied Desmond, looking round to check. 'We can start as soon as you like.'

Terry clapped his hands, gradually the noise in the hall died down, and everyone paid attention. Ron slipped quietly in at the back- in the nick of time, as usual.

'Listen, everyone,' said Terry, as the cast gathered round. 'You all know how important the rehearsal is tonight- we've never attempted to run the show before. There are sure to be all sorts of disasters, but I want you all to carry on in spite of them, so that we all get an idea of continuity. Make sure you know where your props are before we start· and please put them back in the same place when you've finished with them. Now, take five minutes to locate them and check your entrances, and then we'll make a start. After the rehearsal we'll have a quick post mortem and deal with any real disasters and queries.' Terry looked round. 'Is that clear?'

There was a murmur of assent, and the company dispersed to carry out his instructions. At last the rehearsal began, and it got off to a fine start. It was obvious that people were giving of their best, anxious to please Terry, and demonstrate that the show was in a sufficiently good state to be put aside for four weeks.

The pirates sang with a fine end-of-term enthusiasm, and the old horn gramophone caused much hilarity among the girls, who were sitting out front awaiting their entrance. Terry was pleased to see that individual touches were creeping in as some of the cast began to develop their different characters and react together. A few, of course, never would- they would just stand and sing without much animation, in spite of all his efforts, but there was a good nucleus of seasoned performers to carry the scene successfully.

Sheila, as Ruth, sang her song with amusing characterisation, though without the make-up which would render her ageing and rather plain, she looked much too attractive, and certainly considerably younger than Frederic, which would not do at all. Make-up would remedy this, and a greying wig would no doubt complete the illusion.

The Pirate King was magnificent, and got a round of applause for his song, waving the flag emblazoned with skull and cross-bones so vigorously that it parted company from its pole and wrapped itself round Ian's head. This unrehearsed piece of business did not disconcert him in the slightest, though it convulsed the rest of the pirates. Ian was equal to the situation, throwing it round his shoulders with a flourish and exiting behind the King in fine style, to loud applause from the girls.

The rest of Act I went fairly well, with various predictable hold-ups, but the girls did Terry proud with their spirited performance of the opening chorus. He had consulted the musical director, Jack Conway,. about the possibility of interpolating a short section of Charleston music at the end of the chorus music. Jack had agreed- reluctantly at first, but with enthusiasm later, as he saw how effective it was. And the girls loved it- even Beryl and Joan, hitherto so staid, threw themselves into twenties mood- Terry could not believe his eyes. And when Sue came on and sang her song so delightfully, the whole thing gathered momentum. Even Ron rose to the occasion and gave of his best. Then it was Mike Mitchell's turn, and he made his entrance as Major General Stanley with military precision, singing his tongue-twisting number with commendable clarity of diction.

Terry was well pleased with his cast by the interval. Of course, there were plenty of rough edges to be smoothed out, one or two bits of business did not quite work, and the timing of some of the comedy sections needed attention, but all in all the show was in a healthy state. Coffee time found everyone exhilarated, and keen to attack Act II.

'Well done, Sue,' said Ian, handing her a very welcome cup of coffee. 'That song was marvellous. Those high notes- wow! They seemed so easy- were they?'

Sue laughed. 'Oh, they're not so bad. I've done quite a bit of work on them and they seem to be OK- in fact, I really enjoy the song now. I was a bit scared of it at first, I must admit. But wasn't everyone good? Terry must be so pleased.'

'I bet he is,' said Ian. 'But you may be sure he'll find all sorts of things to criticise- that's his job, after all. And however brilliant we think anything is, Terry'll find a way to improve it. He's a perfectionist- but that's a good thing, I suppose.'

'I just wish Ron would layoff the drink a bit,' sighed Sue. 'It's not at all pleasant to act with anyone reeking of whisky. Bad enough that he's far too old- that's enough to contend with.'

'He did sing his song well, though, you must admit,' said Ian. 'Those top notes of his are still impressive-'

'Yes, maybe- but he hangs on to them far too long,' complained Sue. It's ridiculous- Jack makes no attempt to cut him off.' Ian only laughed. He knew Ron would go his own sweet way, re-gardless of the musical director. And the audience would love it.

'Beginners for Act II,' called Desmond, on Terry's instructions. 'On stage, ladies, please.'

Sandra resumed her seat with Terry, and, unnoticed by anyone during the ensuing commotion, the street door opened and a man entered quietly and took his place at the back.

'Why, hello, Fred,' said George, who was sitting near the door. 'Haven't seen much of you lately- come to give the show the once-over? You wait till you see what Sandra's done with some of the principals- she's worked wonders.'

Fred smiled, but could not answer, as the music was beginning for the opening of the act.

The second part of the show proceeded smoothly- that is, until the entrance of the policemen. Charlie Hanson, true to form, turned the wrong way, raised his truncheon when all the others lowered theirs, and finally dropped it altogether. Everyone on stage sniggered, Charlie blushed bright scarlet, and Terry buried his face in his hands. Sandra gave him a comforting hug.

'Better tonight than at a performance,' she whispered.

'Oh, he'll do it then as well,' moaned Terry.

Things were better after that. The scenes with the Pirate King, Frederic and Ruth went like clockwork. Sandra heaved a sigh of relief- she had staged them herself, and Terry was delighted with the comedy, the timing, and the amusing bits of choreography she had introduced.

'You'll be doing me out of a job,' he teased.

'Never!' vowed Sandra. 'Just put on a show with a part I'm suit-able for, and I'll be back up there, taking *your* instructions.'

Then came the tender scene between Sue and Ron. Sandra leaned forward in her seat, watching closely. At the back of the hall, Fred was doing the same. When it came to the beautiful duet where Mabel sings, 'Ah, leave me not to pine alone and des-olate,' tears coursed down his face. He sat there helpless in his deep emotion. It was Sandra singing to him, and all the grief of the past months welled up inside him till he could bear no more. Fred stood up, and stumbled from the hall, unaware of George's curious gaze. The show came to an enthusiastic if slightly chaotic finish, and Terry heaved a sigh of relief.

'Not bad at all,' he said to Sandra. 'Though I shan't tell the cast that!' And calling them all together, he set about giving them notes on the run-through, to be thought about during the holiday break.

'Now, that wasn't absolutely *disastrous*,' he said, 'But there's quite a lot of room for improvement.'

Everyone laughed, for from Terry, this was almost a compliment. Taking the show scene by scene Terry proceeded to criticise, praise or exhibit mock despair at various triumphs or disasters. He was constructive in what he said, encouraging some of the less confident people, and urging restraint on the few who were inclined to go over the top. Everyone paid attention to what he said, for Terry's word was law as far as production was concerned. He was careful to refer to Jack Conway over any musical points, for he well knew that co-operation between producer and musical director was of enormous importance to the success of the show. Concluding his notes, Terry turned to Sandra.

'At this point, I really must congratulate my talented assistant on her splendid work- I don't know what I should have done without her,' and he gave Sandra an affectionate hug, kissing her on both cheeks. Everyone broke into spontaneous applause, and Sandra blushed with pleasure.

'Before you all disappear,' continued Terry, 'For heaven's sake give this show a bit of thought during the coming months. Don't let's have to start from scratch when we meet again! And- everyone- thank you very much for all your hard work- 'Pirates' is going to be a tremendous show!'

A round of applause greeted his words, and everyone began to disperse in high good humour, and in holiday mood.

'Coming for a drink, Sue?' said Ian, and the two of them made their way to the pub. Most people seemed to be heading in that direction, and a hilarious end to the evening seemed to be on the cards..

Beryl and Joan were changing back into sensible shoes from their rehearsal ones..

'How about going for a drink?' suggested Beryl. 'After all, it's holiday time and I feel like a shandy -'

'Yes, let's,' said Joan daringly, already intoxicated with the un-doubted success of her dancing. Throwing caution to the winds. she executed a couple of steps of the Charleston to Terry's utter amazement. Affecting shock at this unlikely manifestation, he immediately staged a mock faint into the arms of an astonished Mike Mitchell, who happened to be passing.

Vera and Gladys joined in the laughter at the scene as they packed away that evening's knitting into their respective bags.

'Been good fun this evening, eh, Glad?' said Vera. 'Like to stop off at my place on your way home for a cuppa? I want to ask you about that bit where we take off the picnic baskets before the pirates come on- I didn't get out of their way in time- nearly tripped Charlie Hanson up-'

'Oh, he trips up over anything,' replied Gladys. 'Don't suppose it was your fault. Yes- I'll come in for half an hour- we can go over a few things while it's all still fresh in our minds.'

The hall gradually emptied. Doreen ran a practised eye over everything to make sure no property had been left behind, then turned off the lights and locked the door.

Sandra decided to go straight home. Recently she had begun to join the others in the pub after rehearsal, and enjoyed the relax-ation, managing to attribute Fred's absence to pressure of work. Tonight, however, elated by the congratulations she had re-ceived from so many of the company on her contribution to the show, she felt she wanted to be by herself to savour the evening anew. There were still improvements that could be made, and she needed think about these while everything was fresh in her mind.

Turning into her drive, she saw that Fred was already home, and that the light in the sitting room was on. Both these things were somewhat unusual, as Fred still spent most evenings at the club, but Sandra realised that she herself was much later than normal. He had probably come in earlier, gone to bed and left the light on by mistake.

Sandra let herself in quietly and went to turn the light off in the sitting room. Startled, she saw Fred sitting in an armchair,. holding in his hands the photograph of her as Mabel, which she had hidden in a drawer. He looked up as she entered, a strange expression on his face, and their eyes met. Slowly, Fred put down the photograph, got up from the chair, and held out his arms. With a stifled sob, Sandra rushed to him and they held each other tightly, in an eloquent silence, the only sound in the room being the tick of the little carriage clock on the mantelpiece. How long they stood like that, neither knew, then eventually Fred spoke.

'Oh, Sandra. . . . Sandra. . . I was *there*- at the rehearsal. . .'

'What? Tonight? I never saw you-'

'No. I left before the end. The scene between Frederic and Mabel. . . . . the duet. . . . Oh, Sandra- it wasn't Sue singing. .. It was *you*. . .. It was you. . . all those years ago, when I first fell in love with you. . . .' Fred's voice broke.

Sandra could not speak. She stood there motionless. It was for Fred to tell her all that was on his mind- she must not interrupt. She broke away gently, her heart racing, to give him space.

'And when you. . . . she. . . came to the words, 'leave me not to pine alone and desolate' - I couldn't bear it any longer- I had to get out of the hall. Because that's exactly what I've been without you- alone and desolate. . . . and I can't stand it any longer. . . . '

Sandra would not go to him or comfort him. There was some-thing she must say before a reconciliation could take place.

'Can you ever forgive me- *really* forgive me- for what I did, all those years ago?'

Fred sighed. Then he looked at her steadily. 'That was in the past, Sandra. We have to put it behind us. What have I to gain from letting it fester in my mind year after year? And whatever would I become without you? A bitter, lonely old man. What's done is done. It was wrong, and you're sorry. . . .I'm sorry. We just have to put it behind us-'

'But it was really dreadful,' said Sandra, tears coming to her eyes and running unchecked down her face. 'How could I have done it? How *could* I?'

Fred put his arms round her and led her to a chair. 'Sit down, love- I think we both need a drink.'

He went to the cabinet and poured- as he had done on that fateful night- two large brandies. He handed one to his wife.

'I'm proud of you, love. You've put your disappointment about not playing the leading role behind you, and you've achieved wonderful results. Let's look forward, not back.' Fred raised his glass. 'To us,' he said, simply.

Sandra looked across at him and smiled through her tears. 'To us,' she replied. 'To us.'

CHAPTER 16

Gladys sipped her second cup of tea appreciatively, and nibbled a gypsy cream. She and Vera had ironed out one or two problems they had encountered during that evening's run-through, and were now relaxing in Vera's comfortable easy chairs.

'I must be off in a minute,' she announced, 'Just look at the time.'

'Oh, never mind, Glad,' said Vera comfortably. 'It's the holiday season now. Are you thinking of going away?'

Gladys looked thoughtful. 'Bert's been gone two years now- and I've never had the inclination to go anywhere without him.' She sighed. 'Not that I wouldn't like a change.'

'Me, too,' sighed Vera. 'I've got used to being on my own after all these years- lots of friends, of course, but no-one really close.'

She looked at Gladys, wondering if she should voice the proposition that had just come into her mind. After all, the two of them really did get on well.

'How about us going away together?' she suggested.

'What- you and me? D'you think we'd get on all right? And wherever should we go?'

Vera got up from her chair and fetched the local paper from the sideboard.

'Wait till you hear this,' she said, turning the pages till she found what she was looking for. 'There's a coach tour of Devon leaving next Saturday week- sounds lovely- three star hotels, lots of stops with plenty of time to look around, and there's even a pickup point in Marleigh market place. And it's not too dear- here, have a look, Glad-' and she passed the paper to her friend.

Gladys read the details and began to feel excited.

'Ooh, Vera- d'you think they'd have any seats left? It *does* sound nice- and I could really do with a break. And I could afford it . . . . It's only for a week . . . Her eyes shone. ' Shall we see if we can go? Will you ring them tomorrow, or shall I?'

'*I* will,' said Vera, determined to act before Gladys changed her mind. 'Just you leave it to me. I'm sure there'll be room on the coach- oh, we'll have such a good time.'

Gladys finished her tea, put on her coat and picked up her knitting bag.

'D'you know, Vera, I think it'd be really lovely to get away- oh, I do hope you can fix it up. I'll give you a ring about eleven, shall I? You'll have found out by then. And let me know about paying, and all the other details, won't you? Oh, now just look at the time- I really must be off! 'Bye for now- and thanks for the tea.'

Vera watched as her friend hurried down the street and turned the corner. Gladys's feet carried her along on wings as she contemplated the week in Devon. In five minutes she was home.

The day after the run-through, Doreen stood in the hall of her small flat amidst a chaotic assortment of canvases, easels, and various pieces of painting equipment. In her bedroom, items of clothing littered the bed, together with paint-stained smocks, a strange broad-brimmed hat, and well-worn sandals. She was off the next day on a painting holiday in the Lake District.

Doreen was no artist, but just loved to slap oil paint on to a canvas with abandon, regardless of results. Doing this in the open air in the heart of the country gave her a wonderful sense of freedom, and she had met up with a soulmate in recent years- Agnes Palmer, a teacher like herself, escaping from the confines of the classroom. The company of like-minded folk, the careless camaraderie, the jolly evenings in the local inn- all these things were like paradise to Doreen, and she revelled in every minute of her holiday. She looked at the clock- time to pack up the car and be on her way. It was a long drive, but she would stop a couple of times en route and be there in time for the evening meal. She couldn't wait to exchange news and gossip with Agnes. Doreen gave a deep sigh of contentment- two weeks of sheer bliss lay ahead.

Eileen and Norma gazed into the window of a small gift shop in Penzance.

'Wasn't it a good idea to call in here?' said Norma excitedly. 'Just the place to get first night presents for everyone- Oh- look at those Cornish piskies with 'Penzance' painted on their caps! The girls would love those- and, oh-' her voice rose to a squeal, 'Don't you love those little china pirates? They've got 'Penzance' on them, too- they're perfect!'

Eileen was not quite so enthusiastic. Her taste differed from Norma's, though she had to admit that the gifts her friend had pointed out were certainly very suitable for the occasion.

'How many would we need?' Eileen wondered.

'One each for the principals- and Terry, Jack and Sandra, of course. And postcards of Penzance for the others- you can't get presents for everyone- that would be too expensive. Oh, Eileen, do let's go in!'

Eileen and Desmond had made up a foursome with Norma and George to tour Cornwall for ten days or so, and of course a stop had to be made in Penzance. The trip was working out nicely so far, for while the two women enjoyed foraging in the quaint little shops, there was usually some hostelry or other where George and Desmond were quite happy to while away the time. All agreed the holiday together had been an excellent idea.

Sandra and Fred, their estrangement at last over, were content just to stay at home during August and revel in the restoration of their former happy relationship. They promised each other that when the show was over they would have a really splendid holiday, and Sandra had already begun to study exotic brochures in anticipation.

'Where shall we go, Fred?' she asked, 'The Caribbean? California?'

'Wherever you like, love,' he replied fondly. 'Wherever you like.' Things were back to normal.

Sue Hebden had been wondering what to do about a holiday, then out of the blue Angie and Sharon had approached her at one of the rehearsals with a proposition. They had booked an apartment in the Algarve with two friends, one of whom had been obliged to drop out on account of an unexpected job change. Would Sue like to join them? She pondered on the idea, talked it over with her mother, and decided she would. So off she went with them to Portugal, and according to the enthusiastic phone calls home, was having a wonderful time.

'Mustn't get too much of a tan,' she laughed to the others. 'Girls were still pale and interesting in the twenties!'

Ian, rather envious of the girls, resigned himself to a couple of weeks at his parents' home at Bembridge, on the Isle of Wight. He could have gone to Spain with some colleagues from work, but he had not been to stay with his mother and father for some time. Besides, the Island meant sailing, which he adored, and his father had a small yacht, which Ian made full use of, weather permitting. There was really nothing he liked better, and after all, two weeks away from his colleagues, whom he saw every day, was not a bad idea. Perhaps he'd invite Sue to join him some time.

Mike Mitchell arrived home late after the run-through of 'Pirates'. A quick drink at the Marleigh Arms had been followed by a passionate session with Sheila in a quiet spot they had both come to know well. It would be much more difficult for them to meet during the four-week break, for Sheila would have the children home, and possibly Brian too, and there would be no rehearsals to use as an excuse for being out late. Mike gave a quick glance in the hall mirror to check his appearance, then went into the living room where Jackie was curled up on the sofa.

'Still up?' he said in surprise. 'Sorry I'm so late- you know what it's like after the last rehearsal before the break -'

'Hi, darling!' said Jackie. 'I've got a great surprise for you- I've just booked us a sensational last-minute holiday on the internet.'

Mike was completely taken aback.

'A holiday? When? Where? What do you mean?' he asked, amazed.

'It's a cruise- Southampton back to Southampton, so no beastly airports- I've had enough of those lately! Calling at Vigo, Lisbon, La Rochelle and St Peter Port- now, won't that be fantastic?'

Mike collapsed in a chair, trying to take it all in.

'It's just a week, darling, so no excuses that you can't get away-you said you were taking next week off anyway, and that's when we go. And- you're going to love this- we've got an outside cabin with a balcony, so we can sip our G&Ts in the light of the setting sun- now, how about that!'

Mike went to the drinks cupboard and poured himself a stiff whisky, not even bothering to go for ice. What was Jackie playing at? They hadn't been on holiday together for ages. She'd been getting very affectionate lately, too. . .. it was all rather strange. He had felt awkward with Sheila tonight, knowing that his present relationship with his wife was now not as Sheila believed it to be. But what could he do about it? Not much, at present, he reasoned. He would just have to go along with it- at least, for the present.

'Another bonus, Mike- I got a very good reduction on the usual fare, for such a late booking. Aren't you pleased?'

'Of course I am- it's just, well- you've taken me by surprise-'

'Oh, you'll adore it- marvellous meals, swimming pool, two theatres, bars galore- just think, Mike! What a time we'll have.'

'Ye-es,' said Mike, staring into his whisky, and trying to take in the unexpected course of events, 'I suppose we will. . . .'

The morning after the run-through, Sheila sat listlessly in her garden, a cup of coffee, unheeded, growing cold beside her. The four weeks ahead seemed like eternity- four weeks without Mike, for how could she get away from the house, with Emma home from school most of the time? Matt, too. He would only be away for a week with a friend whose family had invited him to join them in Suffolk. Brian has tentatively suggested going to the coast for a week or so, but Sheila couldn't bear the thought of leaving Marleigh, where Mike was. At least she could feel he was nearby, even if they could not meet..: or at least, only for a few minutes now and then, snatched from her daily routine. And she couldn't face being thrown together with her husband in a strange place- at least here at home she could find things to do- and Brian would go fishing or meet his friends in the pub. Emma had been on a school trip to France a few weeks back, so Sheila did not feel bad about denying her a holiday. No, all in all she would be much better here at home, keeping busy and counting the days until rehearsals began again, when she and Mike could get away together and plan their future. Sheila thought of the night before, when Mike had made love to her with such passion that she had reached heights of ecstasy she had never dreamed of. Her relationship with him was like a drug now- she could not get enough of it, and the thought of so long without him filled her with despair. But it would pass, and then, in the not-too-distant future they would be together. For ever.

CHAPTER 17

The noise in the church hall when Marleigh Operatic Society re-assembled for the resumption of rehearsals was phenomenal. Everyone wanted to tell everyone else about their holidays- where they had been, what they had done, and all that had happened since last they met. Sheila looked around for Mike- how she longed to see him after what seemed to her like an eternity, but he was not there yet. Not being required at the beginning of the first act, he very often arrived after the rehearsal had begun, unless he had been specially called earlier. It had been more than three weeks since they had met, and Sheila had had no contact with him since then, except a brief phone call.. She was desperate to see him, to touch him, to be alone with him again. Mike, obviously in a hurry, had called her to tell her he had been summoned to his firm's head office in London for a fortnight as they were short-staffed owing to holiday absences. So she had spent an incredibly dull and frustrated time at home, trying to maintain a cheerful front for the sake of the children. Now, perhaps, she and Mike could have some time together, and really get their lives sorted out.

As the hands of the clock approached seven-thirty, Terry, bronzed and beautiful after his fortnight on a Greek island, asked Desmond to call for order so that he could detail his plans to the cast. At last he had everyone's attention, and waved to Mike and Ron, who had at that moment appeared through the door.

"Welcome back, everyone! I hope you've all had wonderful holidays, and spent lots of time going over all we've rehearsed so far-'

There were a few sardonic laughs at this forlorn hope, and Terry continued, 'tonight we'll recap the show, remembering all the things we've forgotten, and probably not putting in anything new. But after tonight, then we'll be on the up and up, polishing, adding detail, brushing up timing, tidying moves and dance steps. We have four weeks to do this- full company on Tuesdays, principals as required on Thursdays. So you see, there aren't many rehearsals really, which means we'll all have to work extremely hard. Is that clear?'

There were murmurs of acquiescence at Terry's words as people realised that there actually was relatively little time to get the show to performance standard.

'The week before the first night must be kept entirely free- don't fix up any social engagements then, for heaven's sake. The costumes arrive on the Monday, so there will be fittings that evening, and also any further individual coaching needed. Tuesday we are keeping for anything unexpected that might arise, Wednesday is the sing-through with the orchestra- usually called a 'sitzprobe' in opera houses, by the way! And don't, anyone, be late, unless you want to incur my wrath- orchestral time is very valuable, as Jack will tell you. Thursday is another full rehearsal, Friday a piano-dress, and Saturday you can possibly have a breather! We get into the theatre on Sunday morning, and set up, light, etc. You will all arrive, put on your costumes, (no make-up) and be ready by three o'clock. We will then run the show technically, adjusting lighting, and the full dress rehearsal as per performance, will begin at seven-thirty sharp. I think that's all. Now, let's start! Pirates on stage please for Act I beginners- with Ruth and Frederic, of course- Pirate King stand by.'

As Terry finished his lengthy speech, Sheila glanced across the hall at Mike, who was talking to Ian. Her heart beat faster at the sight of him. How tanned he was- his white shirt, open at the neck, showed up his brown face and arms- could he possibly have acquired that suntan in London? Puzzled, she took up her place amongst the pirates- she would ask him about it later. Feeling her gaze upon him, Mike gave a cheery wave, and Sheila, immediately disarmed, returned his greeting.

All sorts of minor catastrophes occurred during that evening's rehearsal, which was not really surprising. People missed entrances, forgot cues, fluffed lines, until Terry called a halt.

'This will not do,' he said sternly. 'Pull yourselves together, everyone- the holiday's over. Now, concentrate! We'll start from the

Major General's entrance, and I want to see something that could possibly resemble a show in four weeks' time.'

Everyone looked ashamed.

'Wow!' whispered Sharon to Sue. 'When Terry's on the warpath, it's time to get serious.'

And after Terry's straight talking, things changed. There were still some awkward moments, of course, but everything began to come together, and by the interval he looked more cheerful.

Everyone rushed for refreshments as soon as Act I finished. Ian, first in the queue, waved to Sue indicating that he would get her a coffee, and she nodded gratefully.

'Thanks a lot- I'm parched,' she said, taking the cup gratefully, 'Can't worry about queue-jumping tonight! Have a good holiday?'

'Yes, I did, as a matter of fact- thought it was going to be dull, but it wasn't at all,' replied Ian. 'Went to my folks in the Isle of Wight, and the weather for once was perfect. My father's got a small yacht- nothing opulent, I hasten to add- and I spent the whole time sailing. It was absolutely great.'

'Sounds good,' said Sue. 'Yes, I can imagine doing something like that- I've always fancied sailing-'

'Well, you must come and have a go some time,' said Ian, 'You'd soon get the knack- I'm an excellent instructor! How about you- did you have a good time with that terrible pair?'

Sue laughed. 'It was wonderful,' she replied, 'we never stopped laughing! Just what I needed before confronting the alarming prospect that lies before me! The apartment was excellent- Liz, Angie's friend, was a scream- in fact, everything was really great. I'm so glad I made friends with those two- it would have been so difficult if they'd gone on resenting me.'

Ian nodded. 'I thought they'd see reason when they heard you sing. Look- the queue's gone now- let's get a refill before the second act.' And the two of them hurried off while there were still a few minutes left.

Sheila made her way across the room to Mike, who had been chatting to Jack Conway about his first act number.

'Why, Sheila!' he said, turning to her with a smile. 'It's great to see you- what have you been up to all this time?'

'What have *you* been up to?' retorted Sheila curiously, 'You didn't get that tan in London, surely?'

'Of course I did,' laughed Mike. 'I was really in luck- had a fair bit of free time during my fortnight there, much to my surprise, and spent quite a bit of it by the Serpentine- God, it was hot! And I didn't go home the middle week-end- popped down to Brighton instead with one of my colleagues. You know what the weather's been like- and it doesn't take me any time to get a tan. It's not been a bad couple of weeks at all- except that *you* weren't with me, of course- that goes without saying.'

And Mike put his arm round Sheila and drew her to him.

'Oh, Mike,' she sighed, 'I've had an awful time without you- it seemed endless- '

'Well, I'm here now,' he replied cheerfully, 'all that's over.'

'Shall I see you after the rehearsal?' asked Sheila.

Mike looked worried. 'Darling, I'm terribly sorry, but we've got Jackie's mother staying for a few days, and I don't see how I can get out of going straight home- shan't even stop for a drink-'

Mike saw Sheila's distress, and hastened to reassure her. 'You know we said we'd go on as normal until the show is over,' he reminded her. 'So I've just got to try and carry on as usual until we finally sort things out. Sorry, darling- don't be upset- we'll be together soon-'

Nothing more could be said then, as Desmond was calling Act II beginners on stage, and Mike, who was in the opening scene, hurried away.

Sheila found a seat towards the back of the hall, and sank into it despondently. Seeing Mike tonight, and the thought of a stolen hour or so with him after the rehearsal had kept her going through a more than tiresome day. As the family ate supper together earlier that evening, Emma had demanded a new sweat shirt like her two best friends had, Matt requested to be allowed to stay out till midnight at a slightly doubtful party, and Brian sought her approval of a fairly unsightly DIY summerhouse he proposed to build at the end of the garden. Sheila, her mind entirely on the prospect of seeing Mike in an hour or so, agreed absently about the sweat shirt and the late party, and even managed to express mild enthusiasm for Brian's project. Matt and Emma exchanged surprised glances- it was not often that their mother consented to their demands without argument. They wondered if they should ask for other concessions while she was in the mood to grant them, but decided it might be pushing their luck.

Sheila sighed. Going home to the dreary chores that awaited her without the long-anticipated renewal of her heady relationship with Mike was unbearable. Of course, he was quite right; they had agreed to behave normally where their families were concerned until the show was over and their future intentions were revealed. But, damn Jackie- and damn her mother! thought Sheila despairingly. How long would the woman be staying, for heaven's sake? Sheila needed Mike desperately, and could not have him. She was devastated.

Act II had begun. The girls were grouped attractively round their father, the Major General, while Gladys, Vera and one or two of the other older members, dressed as family retainers, looked on. Sue entered and sang her solo charmingly, and at the end of the chorus, Cyril Higgins, the butler, stepped forward with a silver salver bearing a brandy for his master. Terry had put in a number of small touches for his older singers so that they would not feel they were merely dressing the stage, and they appreciated this very much. They needed to feel they were still valued members of the society- Terry knew this, and made sure it was the case.

As Cyril retired to his place, Vera whispered to Gladys, 'Doesn't he remind you of that waiter at our hotel in Paignton, Glad?'

'What? The one who fancied you, Vera?' giggled Gladys, and the two of them started to shake with mirth, which did not pass unnoticed by Terry.

'Really! Gladys and Vera- have you been on the gin again?' he called out, 'I always wondered what you had hidden in those knitting bags of yours!'

Everyone laughed at this, and the two culprits, unused to being the centre of attention, blushed furiously and resolved to keep straight faces for the rest of the rehearsal.

Gladys and Vera had managed to get the two last places on the coach tour of Devon, and they agreed that their holiday together had been a success. Both seemed to have similar interests, the weather had been extremely good, the hotels comfortable, and they looked forward to repeating the experience the following year. It had helped Gladys to come to terms with the loss of her husband two years previously, and to realise that she could still go about and enjoy herself. With that knowledge, and with her new status in the operatic society, the future looked bright at last.

Doreen had revelled in her painting efforts in the Lake District, delighting in the companionship of a small group of like-minded people. Several lurid canvases stood about in her flat awaiting frames, and she regarded them fondly, each appalling effort recalling happy hours of freedom, far away from Marleigh Comprehensive. She had discovered that the friend she had met on her painting course, Agnes Palmer, lived relatively near- a mere twenty miles or so north of Oxford, and Doreen promptly invited her to the last night of 'Pirates', and to stay for the week-end. Always a loner, it would be a new experience for Doreen to have a friend with similar interests, with whom she could chat, share confidences, and criticise the world in general.

Eileen and Norma, with their respective spouses, had enjoyed their Cornish tour, arriving home with a load of garish Penzance piskies ready for their unfortunate recipients. They had admired the scenery, sampled the local produce, stayed in various farm-house B&Bs, and all voted the trip to be one of the best they had done. They had already decided on a similar expedition to Wales the following summer. But meanwhile, 'The Pirates of Penzance' loomed large. Everything seemed to be going swimmingly, but of course, one never knew. . . .

Terry was better pleased with his cast at the end of Act II. His lecture had borne fruit, for everyone had tried hard to pull themselves together and really concentrate, and it showed. He was especially pleased with Sue, and said as much to Sandra as they sat together watching the rehearsal.

'You've done wonderfully well, darling,' he said gratefully, 'I knew you would, of course. Sue looks so confident- she moves beautifully, and her dialogue is excellent. She even makes the scenes with Ron seem sincere- and that can't be easy. Is he still drinking heavily?'

'Oh, yes,' replied Sandra. 'He's always had one or two before we begin rehearsing, runs off to the pub at the break, and back there when we've finished. He's missing Laura, of course. She got fed up with being left alone every evening- he belongs to two other societies, you know, and he is never at home. She finally gave him an ultimatum, and when that failed, packed up and left. He's very cut up about it- that's the cause of his drink problem.'

The Pirate King, Ruth and Frederic entered at that point to do their scene together, and Terry watched with great satisfaction. 'You've done a great job with this, Sandra,' he chuckled, appreciating some comic business she had introduced. Sandra was pleased. After all she had been through, life was beginning to feel good again.

'Sheila doesn't seem quite up to her usual standard tonight,' she remarked thoughtfully. 'She's lost some of her sparkle.'

'Oh, she'll be fine,' said Terry. 'Sheila always turns up trumps. Probably a bit of post-holiday depression.'

By the end of the rehearsal Terry was quite visibly pleased.

'Well done,' he announced to the assembled company. 'That'll do for a rough run-through-'

There were murmurs of protest at this. 'In four weeks' time we *may*- and I emphasise the word 'may'- have a good show on our hands.'

But he laughed and winked as he said this, and everyone took it in good heart.

'Doreen's given out rehearsal schedules, I know, and I've lots of production notes for you, which I'll give you next time. So, see you then, and thank you, one and all.' Laughter and chatter broke out as everybody gathered up coats, changed shoes, and made ready to depart. Mike blew Sheila a kiss on his way out, and her heart sank as she watched him go. She felt abandoned, and strangely lost. Surely he could have spared half an hour or so, when they'd been apart for so long? She picked up her coat and rushed after him, but was held up by others in front of her, only getting out of the hall in time to see his white Mercedes accelerating down the road. Never had Sheila felt so forlorn. She sensed a subtle change in Mike's attitude, but could not decide exactly what it was. They had parted on such passionate, intimate terms, each vowing that the four weeks' break before they could be together again would seem interminable. Yet here he was, making an excuse to go home early, which she sensed was hardly necessary, and his treatment of her, while not exactly offhand, was decidedly casual.

Sheila was puzzled, and deeply hurt. She could not bring herself to go for a drink with the usual crowd, for she felt quite unable to put on a cheerful face, and laugh and joke with the others. She would go straight home, say she had a fearful headache, and go to bed. There she would lie, unable to sleep, staring unseeing into the darkness, and praying that her relationship with Mike would soon be back on track. A future without him did not bear contemplating.

CHAPTER 18

'Ask the waiter for another bottle,' said Sharon a trifle tipsily, draining her third glass with enjoyment. This idea was carried unanimously, and the order was duly given. There were six of them round the table at the bistro- Sue and Ian, Angie and Sharon, and two new and promising recruits to their band- David Waterhouse and Kevin Cartwright. It was the Saturday evening before the week of intensive rehearsals prior to opening night, and they had decided to have one last fling before the hard work began. The next bottle of wine arrived, and Ian refilled the glasses.

'Here's to Sue- and great success -' he began.

'Hey- wait a minute,' interrupted Sue, 'That's all very well- but I say thanks to Ian- he's helped me a lot by standing in as Frederic- couldn't have learned those duets nearly so easily without him-'

'Frederic, eh?' said Sharon. 'And how much will you pay me for tripping up old Ron at the dress rehearsal, Ian? A broken ankle would put him out of action all right! How about it?'

'Don't even think about it,' replied Ian. 'I'm perfectly happy with my small part- no responsibilities, and a lot of fun. Wouldn't say thank you for a leading role- I'm happy as I am.'

'And what makes you think Ron'd stay off with a broken ankle?' laughed Kevin. 'He'd make a feature of it- work it into the plot somehow. All that matters to him is getting on that stage, hanging on to the top notes longer than anyone else, and receiving rapturous applause! Oh, Ron'll be there regardless.'

'Suits me,' said Ian, and they all laughed.

'Sheila seems a bit down these days,' remarked Angie. 'She's usually such fun, but lately she keeps herself to herself- doesn't even come for a drink most nights. I wonder what's the matter?'

'Probably trouble with one of her kids,' observed David, 'You know what teenagers are-'

'Really?' said Sharon, with an innocent air, 'I was exemplary-never gave my folks a moment's trouble-'

This remark was greeted with derisive laughter, and Kevin signalled to the waiter that a further bottle of wine was needed,

'This'd better be the last,' he said, 'Or we'll have to carry Sharon home.'

Eileen had invited Norma to her house for a last minute discussion about the costumes, which were arriving on the Monday, ready for the trying-on session in the evening.

'What time did they say the delivery would be?' asked Eileen.

'Four o'clock,' replied Norma, sipping her amontillado appreciatively. 'Subject to possible traffic delays, of course. They'll all be hung on rails, of course, which makes life easier. George will be at the hall to help- we'll put the girls in the small hall- more private for them there. The young ones don't mind prancing around half-dressed, but we have to consider the likes of Gladys and Vera.'

'Of course,' said Eileen. 'I say, those two seem to be enjoying themselves in the show, don't they?'

'Yes, they do,' replied Norma. 'Terry's brilliant- the way he's worked with the older members- given them things they can do-making them really feel part of the action, and not embarrassed by trying to look young. And they love it.'

'Wasn't it funny,' remarked Eileen, 'How, just after we decided to put 'Pirates' into the twenties, Boddington decided to put on 'The Boy Friend?' *Two* shows in the twenties so close together! But ours is the first!'

'And it's only four weeks to *their* first night! What are they going to think when they see our show? They'll be furious!'

Boddington was a small town about twenty miles from Marleigh, and there had always been intense competition between the two operatic societies. The prospect of scoring over their rivals by pre-empting their twenties show with a twenties version of 'Pirates', unintentional though it had been, was extremely gratifying.

'The cast have been very good about keeping our updating a secret,' observed Norma. 'I don't believe anyone outside the society knows a thing about it. And the posters don't give the game away at all- it isn't until you see the programme that you realise you're going to see 'Pirates' in the nineteen-twenties.'

'I hope all the dresses fit OK,' said Eileen. 'And that all the girls have remembered to buy pale tights. One or two were having problems getting suitable shoes, but I think they've solved that one now. Anyway, we'll soon see. Desmond and George'll sort out the men, and they can let you see them when they're dressed, and give the OK. Shouldn't be any difficulties there.'

'Good,' said Norma. 'I'll be on my way then, and see you at the hall about three-thirty Monday afternoon. Cheerio, Eileen- thanks for the sherry.'

The few weeks prior to the final few days of costume fittings, orchestral rehearsal and the run-up to the first night had been a strange, uncomfortable time for Sheila. Mike had stayed behind several times after rehearsal, and they had driven their favourite isolated spot in the woods, well away from Marleigh. He had made love to her with a passionate intensity that had almost frightened her, and she was not sure that she liked this new mood, so different from what had gone before. There was no lovers' conversation afterwards, no lingering to talk about their future plans. When questioned, Mike would reassure her that all was well, not to worry- just get the show over, and things would work out. Sheila had to be content with this, but could not help feeling ill-at-ease with the changed situation. Something was different somehow- and she didn't like it.

The following Monday afternoon found Eileen, Norma, George and Desmond at the hall, awaiting the arrival of the costumes. George looked at his watch.

'Ten past four,' he announced. 'Should be here any minute- unless there's been some sort of hold-up.'

'I'll go and look outside,' said Desmond. 'Show them where to park- it's not easy when you don't know the area.'

As he opened the door, a horn sounded in the street.

'Here they are,' he called, and George went to help. Soon the two men, aided by the van driver, were wheeling racks of costumes into the hall. Boxes of hats and other small items followed, and in no time at all, everything was unloaded, and the van was on its way back to base.

'That was a fairly painless operation,' remarked George. 'I hope the fittings go as well.'

'That remains to be seen,' said Norma. 'There are usually a few hiccups when it comes to fittings. Getting Beryl and Joan into twenties dresses will be quite an experience- oh, let's get the racks of ladies' costumes into the small hall, shall we? Then we can match up the hats etc, and put them with the dresses- that'll save time tonight.'

This was duly done, with many exclamations of satisfaction as Norma and Eileen inspected the costumes they had chosen months ago at the hire firm.

'These really are most attractive,' observed Eileen, picking a pale blue, low-waisted dress from the rail. 'Look at these flying panels, and the matching rose at the belt-' 'And here's the hat that goes with it,' enthused Norma. 'It's really lovely- oh, it's Sue's- she'll look delightful in this.'

Once the ladies' costumes and hats were sorted, the two women went to help George and Desmond, who were doing the same with the men's pirate outfits, with rather less success. Piratical costumes were mixed with striped blazers, golfing and cricketing gear, and nautical headscarves with battered bowlers, deerstalkers, dented coronets and the odd top hat. The men's chorus were undoubtedly going to be genuine 'noblemen who had gone wrong', as decreed by WS Gilbert. Finally, amid much laughter, each costume was more or less assembled, and it was decided that a strong coffee was needed before the onslaught of that evening's fittings.

Promptly at 7.30pm the company began to arrive, and soon the girls' hall was filled with noise and laughter. The first trying-on of the costumes was always an exciting event, and this time even more so, as nobody had worn a nineteen-twenties dress before. Doreen, list in hand as usual, tried to restore order.

'Find your costume, try it on and let Norma see it,' she announced. 'I shall be standing by and noting any minor alterations which may be required, so that she knows exactly what, if anything, needs doing. And ask Eileen if you need help with fastenings-'

'That's right, girls- they're all labelled,' called Norma over the ensuing hubbub.

General commotion and giggling followed these instructions, and Norma was suddenly aware of a distressed wail from a dishevelled figure behind her.

'Good heavens, Joan- what *have* you got on?' asked Norma in amazement.

'Well- if this is a nineteen-twenty dress, it's indecent, and I refuse to wear it! I'd rather not be in the show!' Joan was close to tears as she stood in front of Norma in a skimpy frock that revealed a great deal more than it should have done.

'It *is* a bit short-' murmured Eileen, viewing Joan's costume with alarm.

'And much too tight,' added Doreen.

'Come here, dear- that can't be right,' said Norma. 'Let me have a look. . . . .no wonder! That's Angie's. Yours is on the other rack, Joan.'

Joan still looked doubtful. 'But you *said* it was pale mauve,' she persisted.

'Yes, I know, dear,' said Norma patiently. 'But so are several others. Look for a label with your name on it. Sharon, let me see- Good God, child- you can't go on stage like that! We're not doing this topless!'

As she spoke, the door opened.

'Looks all right to me!' said Desmond, viewing the offending dress approvingly.

There were screams from the girls, all in various stages of undress, at this intrusion.

'Go away, Desmond- you know very well this is the ladies' fitting room,' said Eileen crossly.

'Oh, I must have lost my way,' replied Desmond, in no hurry to depart, 'Sorry.' And with a wink at Beryl, who was trying to hide behind an inadequate pile of boxes, he closed the door.

'Really!' said Eileen, exasperated, 'he gets worse!'

Doreen was examining Sharon's dress. 'I think she's got it on back to front,' she said.

'So she has!' said Norma, despairingly. 'Honestly, girls- do have some common sense- look, Sharon- it's perfectly all right now we've got it the right way round. It has a low back, which is quite attractive, and you won't need a bra, with your figure, so there won't be any straps to show. See, now- it looks very nice.'

At this point Angie intervened, looking very attractive in her correct pale mauve dress, and with a cloche hat perched on the back of her head.

'Is this how we're meant to wear our hats, Eileen?' she asked.

'No, Angie- like this!' said Norma firmly. 'Nearly down to the eyebrows.' And she pulled the hat into the correct position.

'But the audience won't be able to see my face-' she moaned.

'We'll sell more tickets that way!' laughed Sharon.

'Bloody cheek!' replied Angie, staring gloomily into the mirror.

Vera and Gladys stood waiting for Norma's approval, both clad in low-waisted black dresses, with white frilled aprons, and lace caps set at exactly the right angle.

'Thank goodness some of you have an idea of the twenties period,' said Norma. 'That's excellent- are you quite comfortable? Nothing too tight? And what about your shoes?'

'We thought that if we wore our black courts- they're fairly low-heeled- and put some broad black elastic across the instep, they'd look like those shoes with straps they used to wear then,' suggested Vera.

'Just the thing,' approved Norma. 'I knew we could leave it to you. Good.' And the two ladies retired, satisfied.

'Beryl doesn't look happy,' whispered Eileen.

'Whatever's the matter, dear?' asked Norma. 'You look very nice.'

'Yellow's not my colour,' mourned Beryl. 'I *never* wear yellow.'

'Nonsense!' said Norma. 'You look fine. Anyway, you'll be made up to compliment the colour of your dress. Don't worry dear-'

At this point there was a knock at the door. 'Everybody decent?' There were cries of assent, and Terry put his head round the door. 'Hello, girls! My, you look nice in yellow, Beryl! Eileen, have you seen Ron anywhere?'

'No- hasn't he arrived yet?' Eileen looked concerned. 'Tried next door?' And she nodded her head in the direction of the Marleigh Arms.

'First place we looked,' said Terry. 'Oh, I expect he'll be here any minute- it's hell next door, by the way-'

'I'll look in when I've checked this one,' said Norma. 'Ah- here's Sue- she won't take a minute, I'm sure- her dress is delightful.'

'Sorry I'm late,' apologised Sue, 'traffic's chaotic- someone said there'd been an accident on the Oxford road, and of course the repercussions go on for miles.'

Norma took the blue dress from the rack and held it out to Sue. ' Slip this on, dear, and let me see you. I don't foresee any problems with it.'

'Oh- is that mine? It's gorgeous!' exclaimed Sue. 'And just look at that hat!'

In a couple of minutes she had the dress on, and there were expressions of admiration from everyone. The twenties style suited Sue's boyish figure to perfection, and she did a few experimental steps of the Charleston in front of the long mirror.

'Lovely!' enthused Norma. 'Nothing to do to that one, anyway.'

As Eileen was checking the fastenings on Sue's dress, her mobile phone, tucked away in her handbag, started to ring insistently.

'Oh, bother!' she exclaimed. 'That's all I need just now. I'll take it outside in the corridor- it's less noisy.'

Most of the girls had been approved by now, and Doreen had a list of minor adjustments to be made.

'Just let me see my three principal ladies together,' said Norma, 'Edith, Kate and Isabel- that's Sharon, Angie and Lisa. I want to see how the colours look, then Terry can come and inspect you all before you get changed. Yes, those dresses look really pretty- pale mauve, apple green and pink- lovely. And with Mabel in blue-'

Norma got no further, for the door flew open, and Eileen stood there, her face ashen. There was a sudden silence in the room as everyone waited to hear what she had to say.

'That was Laura- Ron's wife,' she said. His car collided with a truck on the Oxford road about an hour ago. He was rushed to hospital. . . . . . and he's in intensive care.'

CHAPTER 19

Gradually the full import of Eileen's announcement sank in. Nobody spoke- horrified looks were exchanged, first at poor Ron's misfortune, and then- inevitably- at the impact on the forthcoming show. Eileen pulled herself together.

'Now, girls,' she said quietly, 'Get changed, don't worry about Terry seeing your costumes tonight, but come into the big hall when you're ready. I'm going to see him- and the others, now.'

And she left the room, closing the door behind her. Horrified hubbub broke out when Eileen had gone, and Doreen intervened sternly.

'All right, ladies- I'm sure Norma would like you to hang everything neatly on the rails before you go, hats with dresses, please- don't get things mixed up.'

'Oh, of course!' Norma pulled herself together and jumped up from the chair on which she had subsided at the shock of Eileen's announcement.

'Anyone need help? Come here, Sharon- let me undo you.'

'How dreadful!' whispered Vera to Gladys as she helped her out of her dress. 'Poor Ron- I hope he's going to be all right.'

'What a tragedy!' mourned Norma, unfastening hooks and eyes.

'Whatever will happen now?' said Angie. 'I mean- it's terrible news about Ron, but what about the show?'

'Come on, we'll go and see what Terry has to say,' said Sue to Sheila, who was hanging up Ruth's rather unflattering, but very amusing costume.

Soon all the girls were filing quietly into the large hall, where everyone else was assembled. Terry looked shattered. Jack Conway, who had come to rehearse odd bits and pieces, scratched his head in a perplexed manner, and Sandra sat dejectedly on a chair, staring into space. The cast stood in small groups, either silent, or speaking in low voices.

Eileen asked Desmond to call for order.

'We are all absolutely devastated by the news about Ron,' she began, and a sympathetic murmur greeted her words. 'And now we all have to pull together and decide what to do.'

Terry took over from her at this point. 'It's not a matter of being callous, or uncaring- we are all fond of Ron, and horrified at his accident. But one thing is clear: tickets have been sold, costumes and sets ordered. 'Pirates' has to go on- somehow- we owe that much to our audience. The question is, what can we do?'

'Oh dear, don't you think perhaps we should cancel it?' asked Norma.

'Cancel it? Definitely not!' Sandra was adamant.

'Then, what?' George shook his head doubtfully.

'We could probably borrow a tenor from another society,' suggested Jack. There must be someone in the area who knows the role-'

'How about Greg Bishop, from Boddington?' suggested Desmond.

The whole company groaned at the thought of importing a principal from the rival society.

'That little plump chap with fallen arches?' said Terry unkindly.

'Oh, no-' breathed Sue despairingly.

'He won't do at all,' said Sandra decisively.

'I've always said we ought to have understudies,' observed Terry, hopelessly.

Sue took a deep breath 'There's Ian,' she said.

Everyone turned and looked at Ian, who blushed scarlet.

'You can't learn a part like Frederic in a couple of days,' replied Sandra.

'No, we must get someone who knows it,' said Jack.

'Ian does. Or nearly,' persisted Sue.

'*Knows* it?' Terry was astonished. 'You mean-'

'He's rehearsed with me such a lot,' said Sue. 'To help me learn my part. He knows all our scenes backwards- and Frederic's song, and a lot more. Oh, *do* give him a chance- see what he can do, at least-'

Ian, deeply embarrassed, gave Sue a reproachful look, only to be met with a encouraging smile.

Terry nodded. 'I think we *must*, Sandra. We've little choice.'

'We could do our scenes for you now,' suggested Sue. 'Then you'll see-'

'All right,' agreed Terry. 'Everyone else- you're finished for tonight, but be prepared for possible rehearsals tomorrow, when we have sorted things out. Doreen will phone around. And of course we'll keep you posted about Ron. Eileen will be in touch with Laura. Thank you all, and goodnight.'

The hall emptied fairly quickly. Mike sought out Sheila and put his arm round her shoulders.

'Here's a pretty state of things!' he said. 'We're finished earlier than I expected. Shall we disappear for an hour or so?'

Sheila smiled and nodded. 'Whatever you say,' she said, wildly happy at the prospect. 'We'd better not be seen leaving together. I'll meet you outside.'

Jack was getting out his score and preparing to play for Sue and Ian, for no accompanist had been booked that evening. Desmond and George had pushed the rails of costumes against one wall, and Sandra was placing chairs for herself and Eileen. Sue and Ian were discussing one of their moves, when Norma suddenly exclaimed, 'Wait! If Ian plays Frederic, who's going to be Samuel? I *must* know- the costumes-'

'Cyril Higgins did it in nineteen seventy-eight- he knows it-' said Sandra.

Doreen was not enthusiastic. 'He's getting on a bit. . . . ' she said. 'And he's got that funny eye-'

Terry had had enough. 'Oh, what does *that* matter, for a pirate! In any case, we can stick a patch over it! Now, Ian and Sue- are you ready? Shall we go from 'All is prepared- your gallant crew await you'? Is that OK, Jack? Here we go, then-'

More than an hour later, the committee had retired to Sandra and Fred's house. Although it was after ten-thirty, it was felt that in the light of the dramatic happenings that evening, a discussion of the current situation was essential. Not having been present at the hall that evening, Fred had been put in the picture, and was dispensing coffee to everyone.

Terry sank back in his chair and gave a long sigh of relief.

'Well, who'd have thought it?' he said. 'We've had a prospective principal tenor in our midst all this time, and never suspected it.'

'And a *young* one,' Doreen could not resist adding.

Norma sipped her coffee daintily. 'Ian certainly did sing well,' she said.

Sandra nodded. 'He's a natural. That voice is very promising- and his scenes with Sue have a credibility they didn't have before. Poor old Ron- I'm desperately sorry for him, and wish him well, but he and Sue were an ill-assorted pair.' A sudden thought struck her. 'Oh, my! I'm more glad than ever not to be playing Mabel- toy boys weren't around then!'

Everyone laughed at that, and Eileen smiled affectionately at Sandra, thinking how remarkable was the change in her friend from the dejected figure of a few months ago. Now she could even joke about her failure to be cast in the leading role.

'So,' said Terry, 'It's a unanimous decision. I'm sure, that Ian is to take over the role of Frederic?'

'Unless we go to another society to borrow one of their principal tenors, it's our only option,' said Eileen. 'And in my opinion, Ian is the best one I've heard for a number of years- we're terribly lucky to have him.'

There were murmurs of approval at this.

'He is absolutely secure in his scenes with Sue, of course,' remarked Terry, 'but there's quite a lot to fill in, though of course he's watched the others rehearsing, so he'll have quite a good idea of the rest. And I've no doubt he'll set to and learn the script at once. It'll be quite a rush, though-'

'You've got a bit of time, though, Terry- all tomorrow evening, and there will be other opportunities during the week, won't there? We've got the use of both the halls- that will help,' said Fred.

'What about Frederic's costume?' asked Desmond- 'Ron's so much bigger-'

Norma reflected on this problem. 'Well, they're the same height,' she mused. 'The jacket is fairly loose-fitting, and I could take it in with a couple of darts if necessary. I think I'll call the hire firm first thing tomorrow and ask them to send a pair of breeches in Ian's size, and of course a pair of boots- Ron's will be much too big.'

'Good,' said George. 'Now let's get these rehearsals planned, so that Doreen can let everyone know.'

This was dealt with in detail, giving Ian every chance of going through the scenes he was unfamiliar with, and arranging for Doreen to call the necessary principals early the next morning. Provision was also made for Cyril Higgins to rehearse Ian's former role of Samuel.

Desmond yawned loudly, and stretched. 'Well, that seems to be all for now. We're bloody lucky to have Ian- let's give him all the support we can.'

'You bet,' said Terry. 'That's all we can do at the moment. I don't think any of us need lose any sleep over the new casting. But let's not forget Ron- will you call Laura tomorrow, Eileen? I'm so glad she's by his side. That'll help no end.'

'Of course,' said Eileen. 'And I'll ask her to keep us posted about his progress. We must send him a card from the society-'

'And some flowers, too,' said Norma. 'Perhaps you'd get a collection going, Doreen.'

This was agreed, and at last the weary committee wended their various ways home. It had been quite an evening.

'Oh, Ian- you'll be marvellous,' enthused Angie in the Marleigh Arms when Sue and Ian finally joined them.

'You haven't even heard me,' said Ian, 'You may be in for a nasty shock!'

'Don't take any notice of him,' advised Sue. 'He is going to be really good. But there's so much for him to learn- all those scenes with the Pirate King and Ruth-'

'I've watched them quite a lot,' said Ian. 'I don't think there'll be too much of a problem there. It's the moves- and the timing- that's where things'll be a bit tricky.'

'Oh, you'll be fine,' said Sharon. 'And a whole lot more dishy than poor Ron. Though I'm really sorry about his terrible accident. D'you think he'd been drinking?'

'More than likely,' said Sue. 'It hasn't been very pleasant, rehearsing with him. Maybe, if he recovers fully, with Laura back home he'll change. I believe all this drinking is a fairly recent habit.'

Ian drained his glass. 'Time to go,' he announced. 'No more late nights for me till this epic's over. I've just got to get the dialogue learnt- and as soon as possible.'

'I tell you what,' suggested Sue, 'Why not come round immediately after work tomorrow? I'll help you with the script, and Mum can go through those trios with you- how about that?'

'Sounds good,' said Ian. 'Then I'll be more prepared when I go to rehearse them. Thanks, Sue. Want a lift home? I know you didn't bring your car tonight.'

'Great,' replied Sue. 'Goodnight, everyone- can't turn down a chance like that- a ride in the principal tenor's car!'

'See you tomorrow- they're sure to call everyone,' said Sharon. 'We're expecting great things of you, Ian!'

CHAPTER 20

Production week, for Ian, passed in a flash. Each evening after work he went round to Sue's house, where her mother took him through his vocal part until he was really secure. While this was going on, Sue prepared a light supper, after which they both went off to rehearsal, Ian going through his dialogue in the car. He was overwhelmed with gratitude at Julia Hebden's kindness, and never arrived without a gift- a bottle of wine, some flowers, or a box of chocolates.

'Oh, Ian, you mustn't- it's not necessary- I love doing it!' she laughed.

Having trained extensively with a view to becoming a professional singer, Julia had plenty of hints for Ian, and he was quick to make use of them.

'For heaven's sake, don't sing out all the time,' she advised. 'It's a mistake many amateurs make- professionals would never dream of it. You can't rehearse things over and over again without tiring your voice- you could, God forbid, even lose it. They all know what you can do, so just 'mark' it- Sue must do the same.'

'I will,' said Ian. 'I must admit, I was quite hoarse by the end of last night's little lot. I'm OK today, though. But what you say makes a lot of sense.'

'Of course,' said Julia, 'you'll have to sing full out at the orchestral and the dress rehearsal- Jack needs to get the balance right. It's just the constant repetition when you're learning something that's so hard on your voice. So be warned!'

'Supper's ready!' called Sue, and Ian followed Julia into the kitchen.

'What *would* I do without you two?' he said.

'Never mind that,' laughed Julia. 'But I tell you what you can do now- pour us all a glass of wine!'

Everyone was pleased with the way Ian was shaping up in his new role of Frederic.

'He's relaxing more now that he knows what he's doing,' said Terry to Sandra after the piano dress rehearsal on the Friday. 'Surprising how quickly he's learned the dialogue, and his singing- well! I didn't know he had it in him.'

'I suspected he was worth more than the small parts he usually got landed with,' observed Sandra. 'He and Sue really do make an attractive pair of lovers. Norma's done well with his costume, too. And don't the girls look marvellous in those twenties frocks? As for Gladys and Vera! The other older folk, too- Arthur Dobbs as the butler- you'd think he'd done it all his life.'

'I just hope the sets live up to the standard of the cast' said Terry. 'We shall see on Sunday morning, when we set up in the theatre. Pictures and plans are all very well, but until you actually see it-'

'I know,' agreed Sandra. 'And there are some really dreadful sets about for 'Pirates.' Why do they make the scenery so garish? Bright orange rocks and a royal blue sea- ugh! The so-called designers seem to have no artistic ability at all.'

Terry sighed. 'We'll just have to hope for the best,' he said.

The day of the dress rehearsal arrived at last. The committee, plus a few willing helpers, sat wearily in the stalls surveying their efforts. They had arrived early that morning and set up Act I- 'A rocky seashore on the coast of Cornwall', which, to their surprise, actually *did* resemble that. The rocks were a credible greyish-brown, and the sea pale turquoise, which pleased Terry considerably. Act II- 'A ruined chapel by moonlight' proved to be a bit of a problem to erect until Desmond discovered a vital piece of scenery still outside the stage door.

'Not bad,' said Terry, surveying the realistic stone pillars and stained glass windows with approval. 'Should light well.'

As was customary, the technical run-through would begin with Act II. The scenery would then be 'struck' and replaced with that of Act I. That would then be in place for the dress rehearsal which would follow after a break.

'Good work, everyone,' approved Desmond. 'Let's have a quick lunch and be ready for the fray.'

The Playhouse Theatre, where the society performed their annual show, stood on the west side of the square. It occasionally doubled as a cinema, realising from this enterprise useful funds to keep it going and covering running costs. The auditorium was reasonably spacious, but- as is so often the case- the backstage accommodation was fairly cramped. At two o'clock the cast began to arrive to get dressed for the technical run-through.

Desmond had put a list of allocated dressing rooms on the notice board, and there was quite# a crowd gathered round, trying to see where they had been placed.

'Bet we're on the top floor, as usual,' said Charlie Hanson, peering at the notice to find out where the chorus gentlemen were to dress. 'Yes- there we are- Room twelve- that's up about six flights.'

There was a good-natured groan at this revelation.

'Principal ladies- number two,' read Sharon. 'Good- that's quite near the stage. Let's go,' and she led the way down a flight of stairs to a fairly large room where the dresses were already hanging up- checked and pressed by the hard-working Norma. Sheila was already there, laying out her make-up and wig on the dressing table.

'Nice room,' said Angie. 'I've been in a lot worse.'

'So have I- with more stairs and much less space,' agreed Sheila. 'This isn't bad at all.'

Sue put her head round the door. 'Is this where I am?' she asked.

'That's right,' said Sheila. 'Come and sit by me.'

The tannoy crackled, and Desmond's voice called 'Beginners on stage, please' in grossly distorted tones.

'That's not us,' said Angie. 'But let's go and see the opening- plenty of time to put our costumes on later- after all, there's no make-up this afternoon.'

'Here, let me do you up,' offered Sue, seeing Sheila struggling into her dress for Ruth. 'You're on at the beginning, aren't you? You won't be wearing your wig for the technical, I presume?'

'Oh, no,' said Sheila, 'That's not necessary. And what a sight I'd look in it without make-up!'

The technical rehearsal was, as all technicals are, boring and frustrating for the cast. There was a lot of standing about while lighting was adjusted, entrances tried for access, exits rehearsed so that the cast got on and off stage slickly. By the end, everyone was glad of the tea-break before the dress rehearsal proper.

Lots of the younger ones rushed off to the local pizza establish- ment, but Terry, Sandra and the rest of the committee were still busy with finishing touches and last minute jobs, so had brought sandwiches. Vera, Gladys and a few of the older members were ensconced in the stalls, shoes off and aching feet up, sipping tea from capacious thermoses, and diving into an assortment of plastic bags of goodies. The precious hour before getting ready for the dress rehearsal was to be enjoyed to the full.

All too soon it was time to get back to work.

'Oh- do you do your own make-up?' asked Sue, on returning to the dressing room and seeing Sheila's array of pots, tubes, mas- cara and eye shadow. 'D'you think *I* should?'

'Oh, no,' said Sheila. 'It's just that I've been at it for so long that I've learned how to do it. Anne's doing make-up in room six- just go up when you're ready- she's very good.' And, thanks to Terry, Anne *was* an expert at stage make-up. When he directed his first show for Marleigh he had been appalled at the standard of the make-up applied by inept helpers. All the girls, regardless of individual colouring, received heavy black eyebrows, bright blue eye shadow, vivid pink cheeks and scarlet lips. Pretty girls looked plain, and plain girls downright ugly. Terry changed all this, and now make-up was far more subtle, applied to flatter and enhance the appearance of each member of the cast. The twenties would call for a pale base, Terry instructed Anne. with thin eyebrows, a little rouge high on the cheekbones, and small rosebud lips, Eyes would be accentuated, and plenty of mascara would be required. Terry was most particular about eye make-up.

'If your eyes don't register, nor does your expression,' he insisted. And Terry's word was law.

'Come on, Sue, let's go and get made up,' said Angie. 'Maybe if we go now, we'll avoid the rush.'

And the girls hurried off upstairs, leaving Sheila on her own. A few seconds after they had left, there was a tentative knock on the door.

'Come in,' she called, busily applying a sun-tanned base with practised strokes.

The door opened, and Mike stood there. Sheila turned to greet him joyfully, then stopped in her tracks. His face was ashen, he looked hollow-eyed, and his appearance, usually so well-groomed, was careless and unkempt.

'Mike. . . .. what is it?' faltered Sheila.

For a few moments he looked at her without speaking. 'I've something to tell you, Sheila,' he said finally. 'Jackie's pregnant.'

Sheila froze. She had not heard right, she *couldn''t* have heard right.

'Would you. .. say that. . . again?' she whispered.

Mike repeated the two incredible words. 'Jackie's pregnant.'

Sheila's initial disbelief was followed by a cold, mindless fury.

'But you swore you never. . . . that it was all over between you- had been, for years,' she said in a voice that Mike scarcely recognised.

He said nothing, but stood there, head bowed, not daring to meet her eyes. There was a chilling silence in the room, emphasised by the sound of carefree voices and laughter outside in the corridor.

At last Sheila spoke. 'Get out,' she said quietly.

Mike made a tentative gesture towards her, but she turned her back, remaining completely still until the sound of the door closing signalled his departure. For several moments she remained absolutely motionless, numb with shock. Then the sound of approaching laughter heralded the return of her room mates, and she returned to her chair, taking up a pot of eye shadow and applying it with unsteady fingers.

'Let me see you, girls!' said Sheila with forced gaiety. 'My, you do look nice- I love the rosebud lips- really twenties! Was there a crowd up there?'

'Quite a few,' said Sue. 'But Anne has an assistant who's making up the men, so it wasn't so bad.'

'Mike Mitchell came in while we were there- he looked quite ill- I asked if he was OK, and he said he'd had a bit of a stomach upset,' said Angie.

'We can't afford to lose another principal,' said Lisa Preston, who was playing the small role of Kate..

'Oh, Mike'll be all right,' replied Sheila. 'Nothing puts *him* out.' And she laughed in a strange, mirthless way that made the other girls glance curiously at her.

'Fifteen minutes, please,' announced Desmond over the tannoy.

'Is it time to get dressed, do you think?' asked Sue. 'I do believe I'm getting nervous! '

'Rubbish!' jeered Angie. 'You haven't got a nerve in your body! I wonder how Ian's feeling?'

'He seemed all right in make-up just now,' said Sue. 'I think I'll just go along and wish him luck.'

Over the tannoy came orchestral sounds, re-arrangement of chairs in the pit, and general tuning up.

'That makes me feel really excited,' said Sharon. 'It's not until the orchestra gets here that you feel the real atmosphere of the show.'

Sheila was only able to affect an appearance of normality after the devastating blow she had received because she felt completely numb and utterly devoid of any feeling. Tears would come later, of course- the sudden agonising end to her relationship with Mike would become stark reality, and would somehow have to be dealt with. Meanwhile there was the show to do. So on the fateful night of the dress rehearsal, the principal ladies' dressing room was the liveliest in the theatre; Sheila's jokes were the funniest, her laugh the loudest, her smile the brightest. Nobody guessed what was really going on behind her facade of cheerfulness.

The dress rehearsal went relatively smoothly. There were a few more mishaps: a couple of times the chorus did not keep an eye on Jack Conway's beat, and got out of time, Charlie Hanson tripped over a rock, and Arthur Dobbs dropped his tray with a clatter. Otherwise, Terry and Sandra were fairly pleased. The full company were called into the stalls when they had changed out of their costumes at the end of the rehearsal, for some notes from Terry.

'Well done, chaps- not bad at all. Now, what we need tomorrow is a bit more pzazz! Know what I mean? It's all slightly too careful. .. We need a lot more attack, and energy. That's a general note. Bravo, Ian- you're doing a marvellous job- don't rush the dialogue. And don't upstage yourself in the trio- watch that.' Ian nodded, and Terry went on.' Girls- very good, especially the Charleston sequence. But even here we need a bit more sparkle- you'll do it tomorrow, I know. Nice solos, Sharon and Lisa. Well done all the servants- oh, I *am* glad I decided to have you all as characters in the girls' entrance! It really works so well. Pirates- a little more rough and ready- you look wonderful in all those crazy outfits, by the way- a real scream! Sue- you were gorgeous, of course- hasn't Sandra done a great job? Watch that west country accent, Samuel- it's very funny when it's not overdone- can't always hear the words when you get carried away. Good, Pirate King- careful with that flag- you nearly had Charlie's eye out! And do make sure all the audience *see* the birthday cake when you bring it on, Sheila- take your time over it. And a little less frenzied in the trio scenes- calm down just a bit. Your first act duet with Frederic was very poignant tonight, I thought- maybe a little too much so. Your lines 'My love without reflecting, oh do not be rejecting'- nearly had me in tears!'

'I wonder why,' thought Sheila bitterly. Aloud she said, 'OK, Terry- I'll tone it down a bit tomorrow.'

'Sergeant of Police-' continued Terry, 'lovely, Reg- just the right comedy touches. Charlie- do try and keep in step, and don't look at your feet *all* the time. Mike- a bit more attack in that song- that's something I don't usually have to tell *you*- I expect it'll be brilliant tomorrow. That's all folks-thank you very much. Have a good night's sleep, and see you all tomorrow!'

As Terry finished his notes, Eileen stepped forward and held up her hands for silence. 'I thought you'd all like to know,' she announced, 'That Ron is out of intensive care, and sends his love and best wishes for the show.' Everyone cheered at this news. It was just what was needed to round off the evening.

As soon as she possibly could, Sheila made for the exit, not wanting to speak to anyone. and anxious to avoid being asked to join the others for a drink. Her shock at Mike's revelation, which at first had rendered her completely numb, had gradually turned into terrible, unbearable grief. By sheer strength of will she had managed to keep it under control during the evening, but now it could be subdued no longer. She jumped into her car and started for home, but had only gone a short way when she was forced to turn into a quiet street, stop, and switch off the engine.

'Oh, Mike- Mike, how *could* you, how could you?' she moaned, hunched over the steering wheel, tears running unchecked down her face.

Unwanted visions crowded unbidden into her mind. All the time Mike had been making love to her, he had been sleeping with

Jackie- everything he had told her had been mere fabrication. Sheila began to see through Mike's recent behaviour. He could never have acquired that tan in London- or Brighton, for that matter. . . . had he been away with his wife? Surely not And yet. . . Then Sheila thought of the way she and Mike had planned their future together- the flat in Oxford, the things they would do- the theatres and concerts they would go to- the holidays they would have .... just the two of them. Surely he must have meant it? Sheila searched for some tissues and wiped her eyes, but still the tears came. The years ahead without Mike stretched before her, drearily, endlessly. . . . She thought about his passionate love-making- had he gone home afterwards and made love to his wife, whispered the same tender words, caressed and aroused her in the same way? She could not bear the thought. It made her feel physically sick.

Unknown to Sheila, it was that very thought which began the lengthy process of her recovery from the anguish of Mike's betrayal. She began to feel angry at what he had done- and anger would eventually take precedence over grief. But at this stage she was unaware of this. There would be months of sadness, and a continuous, heartbreaking effort to appear normal in front of the family before she would recover.

How long had she been sitting there? Sheila looked at her watch- nearly a quarter to midnight- she would have to go home. The family knew how late dress rehearsals could end, so everyone would be in bed, and no questions would have to be answered that night. Brian would probably mumble, 'How did it go to-night?' and she would answer 'OK'. Then he would roll over and fall asleep again. That would be all, and she would be left wide awake, re-living that dreadful evening until daybreak. But no, she remembered there were a couple of sleeping tablets left from a previous bout of insomnia- she would take those, and enjoy a brief escape into oblivion. Sheila started the car and drove slowly the couple of miles to her house.

I'm home,' she thought bitterly, as she opened the front door. 'Home for good.'

Mike watched Sheila go with mixed feelings. He had dreaded meeting her at the rehearsal that evening, not knowing how to break the news to her. He had gone home after the technical to fetch a couple of small items he had forgotten, meaning to grab a quick sandwich before returning to the fray. Jackie had greeted him in the hall, a curious expression on her face.

'Well, surprise, surprise!' she said. 'I've got news for you, darling! P'raps you'd better sit down! I'm pregnant. Just come back from the doctor- he's confirmed it. What d'you think of that, dear husband?'

Mike was stunned. Jackie came and put her arms round him, but he felt nothing. He was incapable of any reaction at all.

'After all these years!' said Jackie. 'A good thing we got together again, eh?'

There was nothing else for it- Mike had to show some sort of enthusiasm at this news, so he kissed her, pretending that such unexpected tidings had knocked him for six. Jackie led him into the living room, where she administered a large scotch and soda.

'Poor lamb!' she exclaimed, smoothing his brow. 'What a shock for you- for us both.'

Mike looked at his wife standing before him, immaculately made-up, slim and elegant in faultlessly-cut trousers and exotic flame-coloured sweat shirt emblazoned with the words 'Antigua-land of sunshine'. But his thoughts were of Sheila. How would he tell her?

He had set off back to the theatre with a heavy heart, dreading what lay before him. Well, he'd done it now, told Sheila, got through the dress rehearsal as well as he could, and now somehow had to face the future.

There had been no easy way to break the news- no kind words or excuses he could have made. He thought of Sheila's shocked face when he told her, her disbelief at his unforgivable deception, her dignity when she told him to go. And her courage and professionalism in carrying on with the rehearsal as if nothing had happened.

Mike gave a deep sigh as he reached his car, got in, and fastened the seat belt. He did love Sheila, he knew that, but how much had the exhilaration of their passionate affair been due to the risks they both took, the stolen time together, the constant fear of discovery? Would their infatuation with each other have survived once everything was out in the open? He would never know now.

Mike started the car and drove home, his mind in a turmoil. He would be bound from now on to Jackie and their forthcoming child- the child they had both wanted so much for so long. He must make the best of it. Perhaps life wouldn't be too bad now that this hope was to be realised. Jackie had displayed more affection towards him these last few months than she had for several years, planning the holiday together- which, he admitted, had been great fun- waiting up for him after rehearsals with a drink at the ready, and taking an interest in the show. And they had spent more time together recently than ever before. As he turned in to the drive leading to the block of flats where they lived, Mike found himself becoming more reconciled to the thought of spending the rest of his life with her- and with their child. 'A family,' he thought, 'we'll need to move to a house. . . .with a garden. . . . ' Perhaps life wouldn't be so bad after all.

Mike parked his Mercedes car next to Jackie's Golf, and took the lift up to the top floor, where their penthouse flat was situated. The view from the windows of the living room was magnificent, looking across the river to the town. When the estate agent had taken them to see the flat nearly ten years ago, they had fallen in love with it the moment they stepped through the door.

As Mike turned his key in the lock, he heard the telephone ring, and Jackie answer it. He threw his coat down on a chair and was just about to go into the living room when something in the tone of her voice stopped him in his tracks.

Oh, Simon,' she said, 'You're back, then- have a good flight? Wish I'd been with you.'

'Her boss,' thought Mike. 'What can he want at this time of night?'

Jackie laughed softly. 'I've missed you, too, darling- all this lovey-dovey business at home is getting me down!'

Mike stood in the hall, transfixed, as Jackie continued. 'No, he's still out- one of his crazy rehearsals- won't be back till after midnight, I imagine. Oh, darling- of course he doesn't know- as soon as I suspected, I made sure we got together so that he'd no reason to suspect the child wasn't his! I told you I would- I didn't want to- *you* know that- but what else could I do?' Jackie laughed again- a low, seductive laugh.

'Of course I understand- how's Paula? Not too good? I'm sorry- of course you have to stay with her, I know that. . .. Still, one of these days- who knows?'

Unheard, Mike entered the room, and stood just inside the door as his wife continued the conversation.

'Fancy this happening to us! It must have been that mad night in Antigua- that champagne party- imagine being so careless at our age!'

And Jackie laughed again. 'Must go, darling- he'll be back any time- I love you, too-' Jackie put down the receiver with a smile still on her face. She turned round, and came face to face with her husband.

CHAPTER 21

Sue opened her eyes, sat up in bed and stretched luxuriously. Then she looked at the clock on the bedside table- half past eight! She had slept soundly since midnight the night before, and felt wonderful for it. And what a treat- no work this Monday morning, or for the rest of the week. Sue had decided to take five days of her remaining annual leave in order to devote all her energies to the show, as several of the other principals had done. Imagine doing a full day's work at the office, she thought, then rushing home for a quick meal, and off to the theatre- no thanks! Not with a part like Mabel, anyway. In the midst of these thoughts, her bedroom door opened, and in came her mother with a large mug of tea.

'Your timing is perfect!' declared Sue, taking the mug from Julia. 'I was just thinking I'd have to go downstairs and make it myself.'

'Well, I don't mind waiting on you just this once,' joked her mother. 'But don't think it's going to become a regular service! I'm just off to work- I'll be back about five, so I'll see you before you go to the theatre.'

'Good,' replied Sue. 'Ian's coming round this morning for a coffee- there are a couple of things we'd like to go over before tonight. We may go out for some lunch.'

'Just as you like,' said Julia. 'But there's some bolognaise sauce in the freezer if you want to knock up a quick pasta. Anyway, have a restful day, and I'll see you this evening.'

'OK, Mum- 'bye- thanks for the tea. See you later.' And Sue sank back upon her pillows, her thoughts on yesterday's dress rehearsal.

It was great to have Ian to play opposite. He was a good mate, fun to be with, easy to work with. Poor old Ron- nobody would have wished such a dreadful thing to happen. . . But it did have its good side, thought Sue guiltily.

Mike Mitchell tossed and turned on the bed in the spare room, one ear cocked to hear Jackie leave for work. He had no wish to encounter her this morning, after last night's frightful show-down. There was no clock to see what time it was, but the light filtering through the curtains told him it must be somewhere in the region of eight-thirty, her usual time of departure. But would she go to work that day after the drama of the night before? She would surely need to see Simon- he would have to be told imme-diately of the new and catastrophic turn of events. Mike heard a movement in the hall, then the soft closing of the front door, and heaved a sigh of relief. He raised himself on one elbow, then quickly lay back, his head spinning.

How many brandies had he drunk last night? He couldn't re-member. When Jackie had turned to see him standing there, and realised that he had overheard her telephone conversation with Simon, she had been at a complete loss for words. And after all, what was there to say? Mike knew now that the child she was carrying was not his, that she had connived and deceived him into believing that it was by pretending that her love for him had been re-kindled. She had made advances to him, flaunted her body, caressed and persuaded him back into her bed so that their sexual relationship, so long abandoned, could establish him as the father of her child.

Mike had indulged in occasional affairs throughout the years, as was only natural in the absence of any physical satisfaction at home. Maybe Jackie had, too- the thought had never occurred to him, and probably would not have bothered him if it had. But the present situation was not to be endured- Mike was incensed at Jackie's intention to pass off another man's child as his. Now he realised what had been going on during all those so- called business trips with her boss to exotic places. He thought of Si-mon's wife. Poor Paula- for several years she had been suffering with multiple sclerosis, and though she bore her illness bravely and did her best to remain active, she rarely accompanied her husband abroad. She would be absolutely distraught when she knew what had happened.

So, divorce from Jackie was the only answer, Mike decided, in spite of her protestations and pleading when he had announced this last night. But the irony of it all, the appalling tragedy, was that he had lost Sheila- dear, warm, loving Sheila, who had given him everything with complete trust in his intentions, only to end up with callous betrayal and subsequent rejection. For a split second Mike wondered if he could win her back- but no, he thought, she was too proud, she would never have him after yesterday's cruel revelation.

Raising himself carefully to a sitting position, Mike got slowly out of bed, wondering if a strong black coffee would help. If only he hadn't to do the show that evening- heaven knew how he was going to cope, with his life in chaos, and a king-sized hangover as well. Mike sighed- a long sigh that came from deep within him. He'd just have to manage somehow- he had no understudy, and he couldn't let the society down. With difficulty he made his way painfully and despondently to the kitchen to put the kettle on.

Sheila, aided by her sleeping tablets, and worn out with the stress of the previous day, slept on till after nine am. She was amazed when she looked at the clock, and realised that the house was silent. In spite of the heartache that assailed her immediately she regained consciousness, she smiled. What an effort Brian and the kids must have made to get ready and out of the house in the usual chaos of a Monday morning without waking her! She would never have imagined it possible, and was touched by their consideration and obvious efforts.

The thought of a cup of tea made Sheila get up and go down-stairs. When she went into the kitchen, she could not believe her eyes- everything was tidy, breakfast things cleared away and stacked in the dishwasher. There was a note on the table. She picked it up and read: 'Hope it was OK last night, and you were BRILLIANT. See you later- Emma and Matt'. Sheila sat down on the nearest chair, deeply moved. Tears filled her eyes and rolled down her cheeks. For several minutes she remained where she was, then slowly got to her feet, filled the kettle and fetched a mug from the cupboard. She would face the day by taking each hour as it came. Best not to look ahead.

The time for the first performance of 'Pirates' had almost arrived, and backstage at the theatre there was an enormous buzz of excitement. The curtain would rise in just over thirty minutes- Desmond had called the half-hour, and tension was building up. Early as it was, a few members of the audience had started to arrive in the foyer, most going to the bar for a drink to meet their friends before the show began. The house was sold out, but a few stragglers were waiting hopefully at the box office for possible returns, for a Marleigh Operatic Society first night was a popular occasion. A young reporter from the Marleigh Herald buttonholed George, who was overseeing activities at the front of house.

'I hear we're to see something a bit different tonight,' he said, fishing for some advance information.

'I'm afraid you'll have to wait and see,' replied George, refusing to give anything away. 'Not long now till curtain-up.' He chuckled. 'But we have to move with the times, you know- hope you enjoy it!' And he turned away to greet a party from their rival society, Boddington.

'Come to learn how it should be done?' joked George. 'You're in for a real treat tonight!'

'Oh, we know 'Pirates' backwards,' said Lucy Edwards, their producer. 'We actually considered it ourselves, but it's been done such a lot in recent years- we wanted to do something a bit more unusual. We're a bit fed up with all those crinolines- thought the twenties would be fun, so we chose The Boy Friend.'

'I know what you mean,' said George with a sly smile.

'We heard about Ron Catesby, poor chap,' said Ken Hadfield, one of Boddington's leading baritones. 'Quite a problem, losing your principal tenor a week before the show. We could have lent you our Greg Bishop- he knows all the tenor roles-'

'Kind of you, but there wasn't any need,' replied George. 'We're always covered for emergencies- as I think you'll see tonight. Now I've got to pop backstage- if you'll excuse me-' and, stifling a laugh, he disappeared through the pass door to report his conversation to Terry.

'Goodness knows where they found a tenor who can sing a role like Frederic at short notice,' said Lucy. 'Be prepared for the worst, guys- it'll be a laugh, anyway!' And off they went to find their seats, buying programmes on the way.

A gasp of horror was heard from the Boddington contingent when they looked at their programmes and saw Charlie Hanson's nineteen- twenties picture on the cover.

'They've put it into the twenties!' hissed Lucy furiously. How *dare* they!'

Behind the scenes, chaos reigned. As Desmond called 'fifteen minutes, please!' Jack Conway came rushing from the pit in a panic.

'We've no trombone!' he said despairingly, 'I've just had a message- Tom Watson's stuck on the motorway- there's a queue of traffic a couple of miles long apparently, and he can't make it-what are we going to do?'

Reg Jennings, who was on his way back from make-up, stopped in his tracks. 'My next door neighbour plays trombone- he's in the Salvation Army band- shall I phone him? He only lives just round the corner-'

'Oh, do- right away- and ask him if he'll fill in tonight! He's sure to know 'Pirates'- all brass players do. Thanks, Reg!'

In a few minutes a portly, perspiring trombone player arrived on the scene, bow tie askew. Jack, thanking him profusely, took him to one side to look at his part. One crisis had been dealt with.
In the men's dressing room, another had arisen. Doreen sought Terry, a worried expression on her face.

'Oh, there you are, Terry! Charlie Hanson has turned. up for the policemen with two left boots!' Terry, elegant in white tuxedo, lavender shirt and purple bow tie, rolled his eyes to the ceiling in exasperation.

'Oh, what does it matter!' he said crossly. 'He's got two left feet!'

'He says can he do it in brown suede shoes?' persisted Doreen.

'No, he can't!' snapped Terry. 'Tell him he'll just have to manage!'

Where does he live?' asked Fred, who had been on his way to front of house. 'I'll go and ask him- if it's fairly near, I'll pop out and fetch his right boot. After all, he won't be changing into his policeman's uniform until the interval.' And away went Fred on his errand of mercy.

Sharon appeared, in a state of great agitation. 'Where's Norma? Angie's dress has split down the back!'

Norma, on her way down the stairs, hurried to Angie's room. 'Let me see- what have you been doing, girl? Luckily it's just the seam-'

'I was only practising the Charleston,' moaned Angie.

'Well, I'll just have to sew you into it- goodness knows how we shall get you out-'

'I'm quite good at that sort of thing,' said Desmond, poking his head round the door, to be greeted by a shriek from Lisa, who was standing there in a bra and lacy briefs.

'Do knock next time, Desmond,' said Norma wearily, stitching away doggedly at Angie's back seam, and with a suggestive wink at Lisa, Desmond reluctantly withdrew and closed the door.

Sheila, having finished her make-up, was adjusting her grey wig. 'No-one will fancy me in this,' she observed, looking in the mirror at the plain middle-aged woman she saw reflected there. She gave a wry laugh as she tied a striped apron over her drab, low-waisted dress, valiantly striving to cope with her feelings by forcing them to the back of her mind and focussing all her attention on the show. She had passed Mike in the corridor earlier that evening, and he had tried to take her hand.

'I have to talk to you,' he said urgently, but Sheila had snatched her hand away and walked on as if she had not heard. She could not help noticing how haggard and ill he looked, but she hardened her heart. He had brought it all upon himself, she thought. We're finished. It's over. Nothing can alter that.

There was a knock on the door, and Sandra appeared. She was immediately struck by the familiar atmosphere in the girls' dressing room- the smell of the make-up, the excitement, the apprehension. 'How it takes me back', she thought, nostalgic for a moment. Then she smiled.

'Have a wonderful show, everyone,' she said. And above all, enjoy it- if you do, the audience will! Special luck to you, Sue- I think you and Ian'll bring the house down!' Sue put her arms round Sandra and gave her a hug.

'Thanks for everything,' she whispered. 'I couldn't have done it without you.'

'Must go out front now,' said Sandra. 'I'm sure everything will go splendidly.' And blowing a kiss to them all, she hurried on her rounds.

'Isn't she great?' said Sharon. 'And doesn't she look gorgeous?'

And indeed, Sandra did. She was dressed simply in black, with a diamante brooch on one shoulder, and earrings to match. Her fair hair shone under the light, and she looked radiant. As assistant director she would have to take a call on stage at the end of the show, and she was resolved not to let the society down.

'Overture and beginners!' crackled Desmond over the tannoy, and Sheila checked her costume in the long mirror, straightening her cap and smoothing down her apron. 'Time for me to go, girls,' she said. 'Good luck and- more important- have a good time!'

When the dressing room door closed behind Sheila, Sue looked thoughtful. 'I can't help feeling Sheila's not her usual self, somehow,' she mused. 'I can't quite put my finger on it, but there's something. . . . . '

'I know what you mean,' said Angie, 'I've noticed, too.'

'She's probably anxious about the show,' suggested Lisa. 'She's got quite a few scenes with Ian, and although he's doing so well, she'll have to be on her toes.'

'He'll be brilliant,' said Angie, putting on her cloche hat and pulling it down to her eyebrows in the correct manner, knowing that Norma's eagle eye would be upon them as they gathered in the wings for their entrance.

The overture had started, and a shiver ran down Sue's spine. This was, after all, her very first appearance in a show, and in such a leading role. She knew she must do her best, for her mother was out there, and Sue was aware of how much it meant to her. She would not let her down.

All the pirates were gathered on stage, Ian too, wishing one another luck, and waiting nervously to begin the opening chorus. The overture rose to a grand fortissimo, ending with a jarring discord enthusiastically supplied by the deputy trombone. Rapturous applause greeted this virtuoso performance, augmented by some sardonic cheers from the Boddington crowd.

Terry's idea for the horn gramophone to begin the introduction before the orchestra took over was very effective. It received a spontaneous burst of applause, and from then on the show began to take shape. Ian, after a slightly tentative start, steadily gained confidence, backed up by his colleagues. Charlie Hanson was careful not to trip over the rock that had given him trouble at the dress rehearsal, but managed to fall over a different one instead. The Pirate King had a great ovation for his song, which he delivered with swashbuckling panache, and Sheila determinedly threw herself into her part of Ruth. In her touching duet with Frederic she had to take a grip on herself in order not to break down- some of the words fitted her present situation so aptly. But she refused to let her feelings overcome her, and felt much stronger when the danger point had passed.

The entrance of the girls in their low-waisted frocks and cloche hats was applauded with enormous enthusiasm, and when the short Charleston section was slipped seamlessly into the music at the end of the chorus, the audience went mad. Terry had choreographed the scene brilliantly, with his best dancers doing the more tricky steps at the front, the others joining in behind, and Gladys and Vera and the servants perched up on the rocks at the back, swinging away in time to the music. The response from the audience was tremendous. Sandra, sitting next to Terry at the back of the stalls, squeezed his hand.

'How about *that*?' she whispered. 'Boddington, eat your hearts out!'

Frederic's big number followed shortly, and Ian acquitted himself splendidly, remembering the coaching he had received from Julia, which now stood him in good stead. The Boddington folk looked at one another in disbelief - Ian Richardson was usually just a small part player- what had happened to him? Ian's effect on the audience was immediate. Everyone loves a tenor- particularly a good one- and a slim young good-looking one at that. They obviously wanted to applaud at the end of the number, but the chorus follows immediately, leading into the entrance of Mabel, with her spectacular cadenza. So applause had to wait.

Sue, in the wings, took a deep breath and made her entrance. Everyone was waiting for this new soprano they had heard about. They saw at once that she was young and pretty, but she'd need more than that for Mabel. Could she cope? She could, and she did. Her voice simply rippled over the florid passages, and the final cadenza stopped the show. Now the audience could applaud- and they did, and Sue stood there, a tremulous smile on her face, for what- to her- seemed ages. In the stalls, Julia Hebden's eyes were bright with unshed tears. This was a moving moment for her, and one when she felt anew the loss of her husband. Dear Alan- if only he could have shared it with her.

There was no doubt about it- Sue and Ron, though a rather unlikely pair of lovers, would have got by on the strength of Sue's youth, looks, vocal ability, and the support of the Catesby fan club. But the audience found the combination of Sue and Ian irresistible. Their duet, backed by the girls' chattering chorus about the weather, was applauded warmly, and the two felt they were on their way to a highly successful partnership.

Sheila, watching from the wings, was aware of Mike sitting waiting for his entrance, his head in his hands. He looked up, saw her, and came over to her.

'Oh, Sheila, Sheila . . . I don't think I can go on . . . I'll never get through that song. . . I can't. . .' and his voice trailed desperately off into silence.

How Sheila longed to put her arms round him, to comfort and reassure him. But she dug her nails into her palms and resisted the almost overpowering urge. Her reply was hard and cold.

'What are you talking about? If *I* can go on, hurt and upset as I am by your lies and deception, then so can you! Don't you know there is an audience out there who have paid to see this show? For God's sake get yourself on that stage and give some sort of a performance!'

As Sheila spoke, the girls sang Mike's cue, and with a startled glance at her, he squared his shoulders, strode on to the stage and declared, 'Yes, yes, I am a Major General!' Then Sheila knew he would be all right. She herself was shaking after this encounter, but she was convinced she had done the right thing. To sympathise with him would have undermined her determination to distance herself; moreover, sharp words had been needed to force him to pull himself together and make his entrance. She watched him for a moment, quite confidently singing his difficult opening number, then wandered back to the dressing room to wait for her last brief appearance at the end of the act. The finale of Act I brought enthusiastic applause, and the curtain came down on an excited and gratified company. Sue hugged Ian, Sharon staged a mock faint into the arms of the Pirate King, and Cyril Higgins, who had stepped into the part of Samuel, received a slap on the back from Charlie Hanson which nearly knocked him through the curtain into the orchestra pit. Just then, Terry appeared, noted the rather hysterical jollity, and decided it was time to intervene.

'Cool it, guys,' he said. 'Good so far- but remember-you're only halfway through.'

His words brought everyone back to reality, and the cast, suddenly aware that there was a lot more to get through before they could relax and congratulate themselves, filed off to the dressing rooms, where various refreshments awaited.

'See you in the ruined chapel,' said Ian to Sue and the girls.

'We'll be there,' laughed Sharon.

CHAPTER 22

'Sue, you were brilliant,' announced Sharon, sinking into a chair and putting her feet up on the dressing table with a deep sigh of relief. 'Your song- it was fantastic- and what a reception! God, I'm thirsty-' and she opened a bottle of water and drank as desperately as if she'd just crossed the Sahara.

'It's all very well,' replied Sue, 'but the show isn't just a one-man affair! You're *all* marvellous! Let's have a mutual admiration society!' She sank into the battered armchair in the corner of the dressing room. 'Seriously, though- let's not forget what Terry said- we are only halfway through. There's a whole lot more show to do yet.'

Sharon groaned despairingly, which made Sue laugh.

'Come on, now, remember- you're supposed to be doing this for fun!'

'Yes- and it's time to get ready for the second act,' Angie reminded them. My hair takes ages to do. Lucky you, with a wig, Sheila- I could do with one myself.'

As she spoke, there was a knock at the door, and Norma hurried in to give a hand with the girls' hair. They had to remove their hats for Act II, and arrange their hair in twenties style. This wasn't easy for those with flowing tresses, which had to be pinned up and made to appear short. There had been problems at the dress rehearsal, so the resourceful Norma had made head bands to match the girls' frocks, to be worn low on the brow, and these helped to keep their hair in place. Sharon had foreseen this difficulty, and had gone to Terry's salon the week before the dress rehearsal. She had leaned back in the chair, her long dark hair flowing down her back, and commanded, 'Cut it off.'

Terry looked at her with surprise. 'What- all of it?' he asked.

'All of it,' she replied, with a dramatic gesture, 'I'm prepared to give up everything for my art.' And she giggled, 'Oh, go on, Terry- before I change my mind!'

'Well. .. if you're sure. . ' Terry took up his scissors and began to cut.

Half an hour later, Sharon looked at herself in the mirror, entranced by what she saw. Her hair was beautifully styled into a shining cap, framing her face, and softened by a feathery fringe.

'It's brilliant!' she exclaimed. 'Never mind the show- I'm going to keep it like this for ever- what a lot of trouble it'll save!'

So Sharon, at least, had no problems with her hairstyle, and was soon ready, her head band deftly in place in a matter of seconds.

'Here- let me help,' she offered, seeing Angie struggling with pins and lacquer. 'You should have had it all off, like me.'

'I know,' moaned Angie, trying desperately to achieve the impossible effect of a twenties bob. 'I wonder if Terry's got an early appointment free tomorrow?'

'Give me those pins- and the lacquer,' instructed Sharon, coping manfully with Angie's rebellious locks. 'There- that's more like it.'

'Oh, yes- that's really quite good,' approved Norma, 'Now let me look at you, Sue. Head band a touch farther down perhaps.. That blue does suit you.'

Sue had never worn her hair very long, and had curled it softly for the show, which made it just the right length for the period. The blue head band, which had a matching rose at one side, looked very pretty on her fair hair, and Norma carefully adjusted it to the correct angle.

'That'll do,' she pronounced. 'You look gorgeous.'

'Act Two beginners on stage, please,' commanded the tannoy.

'Here we go, girls,' said Angie. 'Good luck for the second half.'

Sheila was putting the finishing touches to the striking pirate costume she wore for Act II, and placing the hat, garishly adorned with the skull and crossbones carefully on her head. It had to be made secure with numerous hatpins in order to remain in place during the vigorous movement and dancing which took place during her scenes with the Pirate King and Frederic.

'My, you look awesome, Sheila,' said Sharon, eyeing the deadly-looking cutlass tucked into her belt. 'You'll knock 'em cold with that thing.'

The audience, having enjoyed the first half of the show, and fortified by a visit to the bar, were relaxed and ready to appreciate Act II. A round of applause greeted the 'ruined chapel by moonlight', skilfully lit by Terry, when the curtain rose. The comic policemen were a great success, and Charlie Hanson lived up to his reputation by marching down to the front when all the others went upstage. Reg Jennings, as the Sergeant, got an enormous laugh by chasing him up to the back, whereupon Charlie promptly dropped his truncheon. This rolled down to the front again, and a lot of unrehearsed business ensued before the scheduled action could continue. Things proceeded merrily after this, and the poignant scene between Mabel and Frederic, which came later, made a sharp contrast. The audience, sensing that they were about to see and hear something quite special, became absolutely quiet, and the atmosphere was strangely moving.

Frederic has to tell Mabel that because he was born in leap year, with a birthday only every four years, his official age is actually only five and a quarter. So he is still apprenticed to the Pirate King, who means to hold him to his contract until he is twenty-one. Consequently he and Mabel will have to part until he finally comes of age, many years hence. This 'terrible disclosure' is sung to such beautiful and haunting music that the ridiculous nature of its content should be quite forgotten by the audience, and the tragedy of the lovers' parting predominant. That is how it should be, and that was how Sue and Ian portrayed it that evening.

'Ah, leave me not to pine alone and desolate,' sang Sue, with infinite sadness, and the lovers gazed into each other's eyes with such longing that there was more than one member of the audience furtively fumbling for a handkerchief. Terry was no exception, and was openly wiping his eyes at the end of the scene.

'How on earth did you get them to act like that?' he asked Sandra.

Sandra smiled. 'That's not acting,' she said. 'That's for real.'

And so it was. Something happened to Sue and Ian during that scene. They had been good friends for quite a while- since Sue had joined the society in fact, but no more than that. They preferred to go around with the other younger members rather than as a couple, and the thought of a deeper relationship had simply not occurred to them. But on the first night of Marleigh's 'Pirates', something magical happened during their scene together. After their parting kiss Sue had to stay on stage to confront the policemen, but Ian made his exit and remained in the wings, shaken by what had just occurred. He turned and watched Sue standing on stage under the lights, and saw her as if for the first time. She looked so lovely, so very desirable- why had he not seen this before? And did she feel the same?

From her seat in the stalls, Julia Hebden sensed the sudden change in the feelings of the young couple towards each other, and was very happy. She was fond of Ian, and suspected that sooner or later the pair would realise how they felt. And what better time than when playing a love scene together? The show went merrily on its way, and at last the final chorus was sung, and the curtain fell to tremendous applause. The Boddington folk applauded with the rest. They could not do otherwise, for in spite of the rivalry and the annoyance at their twenties idea having been pre-empted, they recognised a good show when they saw one.

As the line of principals took their bows to applause that seemed to go on and on, Ian turned to Sue, took her hand and kissed it. She looked at him, and the expression in her eyes told him all he wanted to know- the magic had worked for her, too, and their new-found love for each other, discovered on stage, looked set fair to endure.

The curtain fell, and rose again, and it was time for Terry's call. To a tremendous ovation from audience and cast, he made a typically flamboyant entrance, took his bow, and kissed his hand to the company on stage. Then he went to the wings and fetched Sandra, bringing her centre stage, where she made a graceful curtsey, and took her place in the line.

'Doesn't she look lovely?' whispered Vera to Gladys, who nodded emphatically.

'We'll be seeing her back on stage soon- you mark my words,' she replied.

At this point, Terry acknowledged Jack Conway and the orchestra, who received their own appreciative round of applause. Bouquets were brought on for the principal ladies, and Sandra received an enormous sheaf of red roses. Glancing down, she saw written on the card in Fred's familiar handwriting, 'You will always be my leading lady.' Her eyes misted momentarily as she thought of all they had been through in the past few months, and how far they had come since that terrible day.

From his position centre stage, Mike looked along the line of principals at Sheila, but she steadfastly refused to meet his eyes. He saw that she was smiling at Matt, Emma and Brian, who were still applauding ecstatically in the third row.

'She still has her family,' he thought bitterly. 'And what do I have? Nothing. Oh, Sheila . . . Sheila. . . what a future we could have had together. . . .'

With a tremendous effort, and with a brilliant smile masking his bitterness, Mike Mitchell joined Marleigh Operatic Society in their final bow.

Printed in the United Kingdom by
Lightning Source UK Ltd., Milton Keynes
137207UK00001B/12/A